Nomography

Theory Redux series
Series editor: Laurent de Sutter

Published Titles

Mark Alizart, *Cryptocommunism*

Armen Avanessian, *Future Metaphysics*

Franco Berardi, *The Second Coming*

Alfie Bown, *The Playstation Dreamworld*

Laurent de Sutter, *Narcocapitalism*

Roberto Esposito, *Persons and Things*

Graham Harman, *Immaterialism*

Helen Hester, *Xenofeminism*

Srećko Horvat, *The Radicality of Love*

Dominic Pettman, *Infinite Distraction*

Eloy Fernández Porta, *Nomography*

Nick Srnicek, *Platform Capitalism*

Nomography

On the Invention of Norms Considered as One of the Fine Arts

Eloy Fernández Porta

Translated by Ramsey McGlazer

polity

Polity Press
65 Bridge Street
Cambridge CB2 1UR, UK

Polity Press
101 Station Landing
Suite 300
Medford, MA 02155, USA

ISBN-13: 978-1-5095-4394-6
ISBN-13: 978-1-5095-4395-3 (pb)

A catalogue record for this book is available from the British Library.

Typeset in 12.5 on 15 pt Adobe Garamond by
Servis Filmsetting Ltd, Stockport, Cheshire
Printed and bound in Great Britain by CPI Group (UK) Ltd, Croydon

For further information on Polity, visit our website:
politybooks.com

Contents

Translator's Note   vi

Grey Alert, Blue Pill   1
The Nomographic Imagination   10
Why Do They Call It "Sex" When They
   Mean "the Ethical Dimension of the
   Doctrine of Relation"?   34
No One's Style   48
Desigual, or Difference   63
On the Norm Considered as One of the
   Fine Arts   79

Notes   117

Translator's Note

Throughout this book, Eloy Fernández Porta uses words and phrases in English. These are often taken from the lexicons of corporate culture or the internet; at other times, they point to Porta's engagement with Anglophone media or index his fluency in the lingua franca of the global art market or the fashion industry. So the reader of the Spanish original comes across references to "infotainment," the "smartphone," the "foodie," and the "fanbase," to "outsider" art, the "mainstream," "normcore," "chaos magic," and the "unwearable." This reader is likewise told, in English, to "Enjoy!," to "Eat well," to "Do it yourself," and even, when the author briefly becomes a "cheerleader," to "Give me an

L! Give me an A! Give me a W!," to spell, "*(All together!)* LAAAW!"

As that last example indicates, Porta's English is often parodic, playful, ironic, or absurd. Anglicisms comically interrupt his sinuous Spanish sentences, or they grate jarringly against the words in their immediate vicinity, to ludic effect. They are like bits of ad copy introduced into an otherwise elegant critical discourse, or Doritos served in a dish made by a chef who specializes in *haute cuisine*.

The effects of Porta's use of other foreign languages – French to signal sophistication, Latin to send us all to mass or to court – can be captured or at least closely approximated in translation. But there is unfortunately no way to do justice to the author's use of English in a rendering of his text in English. "There is no remedy to which translation could have recourse here," Jacques Derrida writes of the "foreign effect" of foreign words used in another context: "No one is to blame; moreover, there is nothing to bring before the bar of translation."[1]

1   Jacques Derrida, "Shibboleth: For Paul Celan," trans. Joshua Wilner and Thomas Dutoit, in *Sovereignties in Question: The Poetics of Paul Celan*, ed. Thomas Dutoit and Outi Pasanen, New York: Fordham University Press, 2005, 30.

Something could have been brought before the bar, of course: the italicization of words and phrases that appeared in English in the original, for instance. But this would have risked confusion, since throughout the text Porta uses italics to other ends. I have therefore left these words and phrases unmarked, although this means domesticating Porta's prose, depriving it of some of its multilingual richness and polyphonic playfulness. All references to brand names, fashion designers, films, television programs, musicians, and YouTube sensations have also been retained, even when these might not be familiar to readers of the English. I trust that this will not prevent these readers from complying with Porta's injunction to "Enjoy!"

Grey Alert, Blue Pill

What if the truly enjoyable act were not trans-gressing a norm but inventing it? What if creativity consisted in pronouncing a law, under the pretext of violating it? What if it turned out that you, who say you prefer the exceptions, only spoke of these because they allow you to imagine the rules?

In these pages, we will explore these disquieting possibilities. Let us see where their convulsions lead us.

Nomography: A collective act in which a regu-lating principle is generated in spontaneous, unforeseen ways, in and through the gestures of a reactive imagination. // A procedure distinctive to an age in which public and private normativity is directly produced by the digital citizenry, while institutions lose their power, become a mere executive branch, or abstain from these deliberations. // A global psychological plague in which the condition known as *normotic* is depathologized and becomes a part of mental health. // A result of the combined actions of aesthetic, juridical, and popular forces. // A form of possession. A perverse desire that organizes personal temperaments, implements forms of order, and creates a common pressure to take distance from heterodoxy. // A form of fanaticism in which the community takes shape as a horde and affirms its collective identity as a *norm-horde*. // A metamorphosis of the social body in which it becomes a regulating force.

"Am I normal?" At a central moment in *Masters of Sex*, the television series, patients of all ages, shot in a sequence of close-ups, look at the camera with varying degrees of discomfort, repeating this question. With each repetition, the spectator feels more interpellated, more like he or she is being given the third degree, more like a culprit. *Are* you normal?

There are some who have responded to this question – which we could also call The Question – with resigned good humor. "I'm just a regular everyday normal guy / Nothin' special 'bout me, motherfucker / . . . If you wanna mess with me, I think you probably can / Because I'm not confident, and I'm weak for a man . . . / And I don't have many friends that would back me up. / My friend Steve would, but he doesn't look very tough." "Everyday Normal Guy" (2009), a song by the Canadian rapper and comedian Jon Lajoie that meticulously parodies the self-celebration proper to hip-hop lyrics, has received more than thirty-nine million views on YouTube. This is more than many songs recorded by full-fledged hip-hop stars, including those who declare in rhyme that they are something special. And if you mess with them . . .

In the fashion show for Balenciaga's Fall–Winter 2017 line, the designer Demna Gvasalia dressed the models in simple navy blue t-shirts – very simple t-shirts, with just one detail added: the brand's name printed in red, white, and blue, resembling the logos used in North American electoral campaigns. It was not this political connotation that interested Gvasalia, though. It was instead the appropriation of a garment that, defying the rules of the brand, was common, even cheap, and cut across divisions of class. Rather than granting distinction to its wearers, the t-shirt unified them. The brand that practically invented glamor thus filled the runway with bodies that, each in its own modest t-shirt, seemed not to belong to fashion world professionals, but rather to be the bodies of humble, naive, dedicated voters. This was a fall from high fashion to plain old voting.

A long shot shows a heavily trafficked street. Cars, pedestrians coming and going, a busy routine. Everything's uneventful. The spectator sees all of this, waiting in vain for some incident, an accident, a cut in the digital programming, or an emergence of the Lacanian real. No such thing happens. The use of security footage in exhibition spaces, pioneered by Michael Snow, who is also Canadian, has become so widespread in video art that it is now a recurring trope in galleries and museums: the unedited, unaltered record of the ordinary.

Live show! Come see the commonplace! It's happening right now!

Super normal. What a strange oxymoron. . . . And yet it has done well lately. We find it in

4

a book-length essay about interior design that celebrates that tranquil beauty of Italian coffee machines and rubber boots. It is also the name of a refined design studio. The phrase glows, in red neon, on the façade of a Japanese restaurant in Melbourne. Meanwhile, another phrase, *Kid Normal*, provides the title of a celebrated series of children's books whose protagonist is made special precisely by his lack of superpowers, or rather by his gradual discovery, during the course of many adventures, that the greatest gift, the real gift from the gods, is . . . being, unlike other superheroes in pajamas, just another kid. One of many.

"No International Norm Regulates This Type of Gestation." This headline in *El País*, Spain's most widely read newspaper, confronts the reader with the apocalyptic threat of a complete lack of organizing principles. "Sixteen Unwritten Rules That All Peoples Respect." A story in the paper's travel section lists dos and don'ts for "rural Spain" – a fictional realm conjured up by a metropolitan, centralist mindset. Chaotic deregulation and customary normativity thus constitute two guiding frameworks, two ways of negotiating two different territories: the global jungle and the local landscape. Globalizing processes turn the planet back into a *terra incognita*, rocked by the fluctuations of financial markets and the witchcraft of Bitcoin. Here we are in need of a new breed of adventurers, discoverers equipped with dried meats and bearing constitutions, ready to raise the flag of Law in lawless lands. By contrast, in provincial spaces, where customs are hypercodified, familiarity is defined by the ability to learn autochthonous customs and local colors. Hence the emergence of a sort of globalized regionalism.

The biggest music festivals advertise themselves using the hashtag #TheNewNormal, and even surprise parties are supposed to be organized according to sets of rules. A National Consortium of Unification, made up of the apostles of *normativité*, establishes rules for coexistence, in tumultuous meetings where the recounting of rapid-fire fables is the order of the day. This absurdist fiction, imagined by Boris Vian, has become the stuff of our times.[1]

Now books of poetry begin this way:

I have a friend who tells me that she only
wants to be a normal girl, but she often changes

her mind and keeps acting strangely, which I like
and admire.

(Specifically when it comes to indecision and the
refusal to compromise.)[2]

Biopolitical struggles become disputes over
the identification of gender's unwritten rules and
efforts to lay claim to the exceptions:

Are you asking me, Ma'am, whether it is normal to
be heterosexual? Of course! Just as it is normal to
be homosexual![3]

. . . but this incorrect perception – this deliber-
ately incorrect perception – of a new relational
order in which the traditional order would be
inverted is in fact refuted in various spaces within
the queer community, where this dichotomy is
reinscribed in the disjunction between assimilation and singularization, between the dissolution
of singularity and its preservation.[4]

*A world that has not yet died and another that
is still being born: we are living in the historical
moment of a transition from the denaturaliza-
tion of heterosexuality to the social consolidation of
non-normative sexualities. This is also a transition*

from one paradigm that is dissolving (giving rise to nostalgias, laments, and regressive and reactionary movements) to another, emergent phenomenon that is trying to establish itself (and that is continually attacked by those who confuse it, or pretend to confuse it, with a new paradigm).

Now books of poetry end this way:

I believe in reevaluating my sexual identity
as a new vocabulary emerges.[5]

Could this be the new specter haunting the world? A homogenizing force? A claim that *we are all the same*, pronounced in a tiresome and despondent way? A becoming-normal? How has this happened? Didn't they tell us that we were living in the age of shifting identities, of proliferating subjectivities, of a plethora of personalities? Haven't the affects, sexuality, and technology teamed up, in a triumphant triumvirate, to confer on each body its singularity and on each individual her transformations and renunciations, his undoing [*contra-devenir*] of gender, class, and occupational destiny? From what foul maze of cubicles and grids do these forces emerge, these forces that lead even those who are changeful by nature

– children, musicians, fashionistas, the freest of free spirits, those who play at life and play their lives as if on a multicolored chessboard – to end up in the greyest square?

The Nomographic Imagination

Creativity and Liberalism

The centralizing processes of *normalisation*, which originated in France in the eighteenth century and were crucial to the construction of the modern European nation-states, unfold in new ways in a changing, globalized context characterized by an interplay between national identities and multinational, corporate commerce.

Homogenization, leveling, depersonalization: these are the terms used by cultural criticism to explain the processes through which individuality has been blurred, in a sense, because of the pressures exerted by leveling apparatuses. The media, the influence of the group on the individual, and fashion have often been described as mechanisms poised to deprive the ego of its experiences, opinions, and feelings. It would be useless to deny that these three apparatuses have this capacity or that they employ it continually. But this is not the only capacity they have and employ. Conversely, to suggest that the practices that we tend to recognize as means of subjectivation – for instance, practices relating to sexuality, love, or poetry – are *always* and *only* means of subjectivation would be to lapse into a sort of ornamental idealism. Depending on the circumstances, these practices can be expressive, but they are also denotative. They promise freedom at the cost of adherence to convention, whether this convention takes the form of the missionary position, the declaration of love, or the hendecasyllable. To spend time in these three realms – the sexual, the amorous, or the poetic – is to see people who differ from one another in their ethnicity, family background, psychology, and character act in similar, even interchangeable, ways in bed, give voice to their feelings in very similar tones, and compose verses that, if left unsigned, could be attributed to other authors. There is no subjectivating force in poetry that is not also in the media. There are no more limits in fashion than there are in sex.

The notion of "normality" seems to us like an empty center around which experiences and areas of knowledge are structured. This notion does not usually allow for rigorous definition, which does not prevent it from occupying a central place in the imaginary that we use to organize our lives. It is an idea that is as evanescent in the realm of theory as it is constitutive in the realm of cognition. From the field of neurology, we have learned that this is a mythic and reductive concept that results from the confusion of *model* behaviors with those that seem to us to be *habitual* or *representative*.[1] In psychiatry, the old definitions linked to policing were given up as the field yielded to a functionalist vision, according to which feelings can be considered normal to the extent that they perform *beneficial and functional* tasks, allowing the individual to express him- or herself and establish bonds.[2] For their part, philosophies of subjectivity always have to concede that there is a difference between a real subject and an imaginary set of attributes. It hardly matters whether this distinction is defined as a triumph or a failure; in either case, *the polarity that separates normalizing forces from subjectivating apparatuses must be called on in order for an ego to be constituted.*

This polarity is based on the understanding of the norm that had its origins in Jewish thought, articulated in the late nineteenth century in the sciences of the psyche. From this perspective, the norm is defined first and foremost as a limit. The expressive subject would end there where the norm begins. Whoever transgresses the norm becomes subject to the police and the law; lifeless, he or she is at the mercy of these powers. But this idea, which is very widespread, overlooks several key attributes of the norm. First, it fails to recognize the *expressive capacity* that is offered to those who are detained and interrogated, and not only to free subjects. Second, this account of the norm ignores the *self-consciousness* that the interrogating authority elicits. In Judith Butler's terms, it is under the pressure of the law that a subject capable of reflexivity emerges. And this reflexive movement gives rise to a sort of creativity whose subjective implications are inextricably tied to normativity. This could be called a *ludic capacity*, in a specific sense of "ludic," distinct from what this word means when it refers to *homo ludens*.

In this sense, "play" is not the opposite of seriousness, but rather the opposite of "obscurity." Because the field of play is the only realm in which rules are clear. This differentiates it from the rest of reality, which is unregulated, dispersed in an inscrutable instruction manual. The pages of this book, written on the sand, address various themes, which alternate according to who knows what logic: the constants that govern the fluctuations of the stock market, the rules of politeness in a small East Asian city, the rules according to which a would-be lover improvises as he makes his way in matters of love, and those that determine even the most thoughtless movements in a game of four-player chess.

Why are norms obeyed? The most pragmatic explanation is offered by theories of power: because there is no other option; because to be a citizen is to be a subject. But this response does not explain why so many people behave like subjects without for all that feeling subjugated. More importantly: this response cannot account for how, from this subaltern position, people come to comprehend even unwritten laws. This last question has been addressed in the field of moral philosophy. From this perspective, norms are first of all *responses*. And they emerge because we constantly find ourselves in situations that raise normative questions. The cognitive understanding of norms should be complemented with another that we might call "appearance-based." We can see the force of appearance at work in those cases where an informal linguistic proposition or an implicit idea gives rise to acts of obedience *because the latter appear to be norms*:[3] that is, because they do not seem to be opinions or occurrences and are distinct from pieces of advice or proposals.

What economic system could take advantage of and realize the expressive and creative potentials of the norm? On this point, we find that sociological studies of subcultures are tellingly in agreement with studies in the field of aesthetics. In the former field, scholars have identified the figure of the creator of norms, who has been defined as a sort of *moral entrepreneur*. Entrepreneurship in business is associated with the attitude of the reformist "crusader" who presents him- or herself as a professional discoverer of errors.[4] This dual role is characteristic of the liberal system, so much so that it suggests a correlation between the mindset that emerges from liberalism, on the one hand, and, on the other, the transgressive legitimacy of the artistic practices of the avant-gardes.[5]

GAOLER: I realize you when I tell you who you are. I realize you by judging you.[6]

The relativist process of *paideia* promises a subjectivity without limits – as in claims like, "every body is a world"; "I'm different from others, as is everyone"; "sexual orientation isn't a destiny but rather a sort of drift, plural, unpredictable, and open to suggestion." This process corresponds to a strategic extension of the field of the normative and thus to the attribution of nomographic capacities to the citizen. In this simulacrum of liberal democracy, in which anyone can spontaneously become a lawgiver, the media and its publics have traded places. Traveling along the yellow river of sensationalism, the media offer up instant anomalies in every newscast, events tailormade to be replayed and retweeted. Prosumers then *consume* these doses of anomaly, and they *produce*, by means of complaints, demands, or Change.org petitions, proposals for regulating the anomalous.

In this way, pseudo-juridical responsibilities are delegated to the public; users are given the power to act as a sort of tribunal. When real intellectuals turn to the media, appealing to the media's judgments to protest, they miss the mark; the media only produce events, accompanied by a footnote or two, official and authorized. The event is not a legal process; the only authentic parallel system of justice is *the legalism of the prosumer.*

What's Done Is Law[7]

The rise of the law of the prosumer confirms a number of sociological theses. Devised in the context of an effort to address the forms of polarization that I have been commenting on, these theses effectively shifted the field's focus from the role of major state mechanisms to the part played by citizens.[8] In a new way, sociologists also began to pay attention to the function of communication. Making statements, denouncing, and sharing denunciations are all speech acts and forms of digital writing that axiologically construct the individual, affirming understandings shared with others and establishing new shared understandings.

The body defined as normalized and normalizing is not, as in the dystopias of the twentieth century, a matter of repressed physicality or a clone. On the contrary: as we know, this body's materiality is determined by imaginary attributes, ideas held in common. Our understanding of the body is, in this sense, more *imaginative* than other, earlier versions of corporeality. This imaginary is the product of two apparatuses that connect its interior to its exterior: psychology and law. From the point of view of the sciences of the psyche, the body's most distinctive trait is a *normopathic compulsion* – that is, an unstoppable impulse to seek, in the world around it, anomalies that let it loudly proclaim regulating principles. For a body that is affected by normotic conditions, or indeed constituted by them, reality is a highway that has been badly paved, that is marked by potholes that have to then be covered one by one, in a labor of leveling or polishing. This compulsion can be understood as one of the "pseudo-normal" conditions generated in a desperate response to a crisis of adaptation.[9] Adapting – by force – to new media, to new geopolitical fault lines, to the dissolute and ever-shifting state of digital, financial affairs.[10] This experience of a permanent change gives rise to a reflex to slow it down, or at least an effort to control its rhythm by loudly proclaiming an inalienable principle. The repeated act of proclamation functions as a way of marking time, a sort of verbal bridge between past and future. This is a technique without guarantees: anyone who pronounces the *word of the law* always does so desperately. An eternal doubt is lurking: will the law remain in force? Will the rule that I now invoke end up being violated?

The psyche is an apparatus ruled by an ordering principle known as the "superego." The law appears to us as the exterior form taken by the superego or as its projection onto the surfaces of institutions. This correlation has been developed in the context of the French tradition of the philosophy of law, with its origins in the work of Georges Canguilhem. In Canguilhem's work, the concept of the prohibitive norm is replaced by another, more productive concept: that of the "normative project." This project is not only a matter of exclusion; "rather, it is always linked to a positive technique of intervention and transformation."[11] In the background of this project, and motivating it, there is undoubtedly a desire for control, but also a "need, obscurely felt by society,"[12] to see its acts of obedience, to ensure that these are seen as meritorious, and to guarantee that those who err will not be forgiven.

In this context, normalization can be understood as a leveling operation but also as *a product of the aesthetic imagination*. The most extreme version of this idea can be found in the notion of *the force of law* elaborated in the deconstructive critique of law. Here the force of law is defined as an "order that defines itself as an absolute, absolute and detached from every origin."[13] The foundational moment of law-making thus takes place outside the law. It is an act of madness; nothing grounds it, and it can only be considered a "subversive law." This brings law into relation with fictional creation, with literature, whose history depends on myths of origin. Performative and always under construction, the work of art of the norm unfolds as "an enormous prejudgment in the form of a paradoxical denial in respect of judgment itself."[14]

Where does this happen? Theories that respond to this question are topographical: they imagine a symbolic space in which law is made present or one that shines in its absence. Canguilhem drew a distinction between two types of imagined, pre-normative spaces: the golden age and the age of chaos. These are places or utopias, non-places, where reality, lacking an efficient cause, persists in an insubstantial, diffuse state. Hence the *Metamorphoses*, whose most distinctive trait is not their changeful marvels, but rather the clamorous absence of all regularity in them. Where there is no repetition, there can be no habit. Laurent De Sutter invokes the second of Ovid's *Metamorphoses* in order to indicate how, in the absence of credible foundations, the law is always proposed as a solution to chaos. But "the hypothesis of chaos *is* chaos itself."[15] The panorama that shows the unregulated world is – and can only be – fictional, hyperbolic, a work of apocalyptic literature based on real events.

This spatial nature of the norm has been elaborated in queer theory from two complementary perspectives: that of psychology and that of urbanism. Lauren Berlant has characterized normativity as a "resting place" for the fantasy of "a simple life," freed from the complications of the ordinary, in particular those that are derived from sexual behavior. Conforming to normative desires would thus constitute a kind of *posture*: a form of convenience or a way of reclining, a place where one can – finally – be comfortable.[16] A critique of this fantasy has emerged within urban studies, which show how, in processes of pinkwashing and gentrification, sexual difference is recodified, converted into a marketing strategy, and strategically localized in areas where corresponding patterns of consumption are configured, in keeping with standardizing criteria driven by class scripts.[17]

According to this logic, *the norm does not precede the case of its application and does not merely cover it with the letter of the law.* Nomographic corporeality makes codes adapt to actions and events that take place at the physical level, so that "facts," things done, "become laws," as José Luis Pardo puts it.[18] Under a compulsive law that governs on this kind of case-by-case basis, the citizen only aspires to *set a precedent*: he or she wants to see his circumstances elevated to the status of an original case in the new penal dispensation. Power over the citizen's own body will be conceded – but only if the citizen pays the price. To guarantee this power, the law will have to be reinvented time and again, to account for bodily heterodoxies in its legislative taxonomy. We hear a lot of talk about emancipated bodies, but this libertine promise *in fact* directly leads to the imposition of new rules in the speculative game called "freedom." Thus only one body has managed to extend itself beyond its limits: the body of the Law, the legislative *corpus*.

Enjoy!

There is no imagination without enjoyment. And what kind of enjoyment is extracted in the exercise of juridical and entrepreneurial powers? Could it be, as Canguilhem suggests, that one can enjoy the value of the rule itself? Yes, as long as it has been "subjected to the test of dispute."[19] Enjoyment of the act of disputation is accompanied by a sexual tension: the tension that, for instance, parents cause when they try in vain to prevent their children from masturbating.[20]

Enjoyment of the norm prevails over sexual enjoyment. The latter, formerly considered to be the pinnacle of our bodily capacity, now loses its integrity and credibility due to its apparent deregulation. Sexual behavior has gradually ceased to be one of the sources of personal character. In this way, a change has taken place in the procedures used to characterize the individual.

The description of sensual singularity moves onto another plane when it confronts the emergence of a political subject whose claims take the form of demands addressed to a chorus, demands for the fulfillment of an ethical principle relating to intimate practices. On an informal level, often on social media, we see an enjoyment in the compulsive gesture of pointing to a place of deviation and bombarding it with tweets. On the formal level, in the street, we see a collective, indignant enjoyment in the demand for a normative project,[21] whether this takes the form of rules for addressing others (compliments), rules governing sex itself (consent), or rules related to its consequences (as in the case of abortion). Abortion laws that once seemed irreversible are violated (as in Nicaragua), rejected (as in Argentina), or called into question (as in Texas, where certain politicians who were children in 1985 seem never to have gotten over the experience of seeing *Back to the Future*, since they continue to search for a time machine capable of returning us to that year).

Whenever the word "diversity" is pronounced, someone is being told: *you are in the world because it takes all kinds*. Sexual pluralism gives rise to a kind of Cartesian madness, an effort to name and codify all fledgling identities. And this effort in turn gives rise to a growing anxiety: might the social body itself be on its way to becoming – or might it have already become – polymorphously perverse? This fear is not the exclusive province of right-wing ideologies. Left-wing media try to locate it on the right in order to assuage their own anxieties. In particular, they seek to minimize the fear that the body that demonstrates politically is incompatible with the body that participates in orgies, that militancy cannot be multi-orgasmic. As Jean Maisonneuve has noted, an elusive body gives rise to an ineluctable form of rule that seeks to minimize the threat of chaos by reducing the source of physical agitation to collective stereotype: "[A]s soon as a taboo relating to the body is relaxed or fades away in favor of a lax eclecticism, or an exhibitionism, the symbolic weight of transgression and of sexual difference is diminished. For this reason, it seems that in any case a certain rule persists or is promoted."[22] And conversely: a norm that is imprecise or elusive gives rise to a form of genitality that is inescapably regulated. Norms seem to be rigid, but they do what they want. When it comes to the genitals, we have made them responsible for representing desires, wild parties, and unleashed impulses. But – poor things – they merely do what they can.

Try it yourself, acting in concert with your fellow citizens – or in complicity with your fellow petitioners. Make your own norms, engage in your own, original forms of censure, in creative roundups, searches and seizures, detentions. Everybody wants to be Zapruder. Every god is working with the police. A drive propels us through every experience, prompting us to regard customs as suspect, to punish other people's linguistic errors, or to produce elaborate readings of body language that take the form of gifs. All forms of personal relations are considered dysfunctional by default. Reciprocal vigilance leads to the creation of an aesthetic regime in which the divine eyes of video surveillance systems are retrofitted in a gaze that is human, all too human. Nokia and Samsung become weapons manufacturers.

On the Tempered Passions

It is an ancient and a grave error to associate normality with dispassion. And a corollary of this error follows from its projection onto the gender binary, situating masculinity on the side of cold dispassion, sentimental atonality, emotional illiteracy, or stoicism defined as a sort of empathic deficit, an inability to undertake emotional self-analysis or sympathize with others, especially women, in an intimate way. This is an idea that everyone has: men and women, straight and LGBTQ+ people alike have all collaborated in the daily construction of this idea, its reaffirmation and retrofitting. They have all pointed to and denounced the most recent symptoms of this supposed pathology, this reluctance to engage with, or this outright denial of, the passions.

This broad agreement suspends the differences between gendered spaces and perspectives as well as those determined by sexual orientation. Satirical comic strips are often drawn by men in corners of the publishing world where the air is thick with testosterone. The foundational theses of Second Wave feminism were developed in university offices and in communes run by artists, where sorority acquired a particular political valence. Reasonable and reasoned deconstructions of the myths of masculinity are written, published, and performed in places where queer sociability has displaced and marginalized personal relationships based on complicity with butch hetero masculinity. These are all very different subcultural scenes and architectural spaces, but despite the differences in their various terminologies, the conclusions that their occupants reach are comparable, sometimes even identical. These conclusions converge on the image of a traditional Man, son of Vitruvius and of *Playboy*, who is a specialist in spark plugs and engines. He says:

> Look at me with my big fat car, and check out the sweet tune-up I've given it. But my nights are agitated. I wake up covered in sweat because of a recurring nightmare. In it, the car has sprung a leak and is *losing oil* . . .

This man knows nothing of the passions and can only cry when the goalie of his masculine values makes a mistake, when, although he reaches for it with a pointless – and slightly effeminate – dive, the ball finds its way into the goal that he's defending, after a shot taken by Jack Halberstam or one of those other, free-floating strikers who move so well between the lines, shuttling between the men's and women's lanes, incredible dribblers who evade the stolid defenders, who bypass the sturdy fullbacks, who shoot, in the end, unplayable shots from outside the box of gender.

The differences between the three perspectives that I have mentioned are more stylistic than conceptual. In the vignette involving the creators of comic strips, the butch man responds, with familiar, virile stubbornness, to the sophisticated emotional reasoning of a woman. In the feminist manifesto, the Man, a character created by the gendered imagination, is built organ by organ – but does he, in fact, have more than one? He is the sum of his negative qualities. He's in the red. A propositional addendum for a post-gender society, this Man has become History. He is like the triceratops or Sanskrit, and only viriloid female spirits survive, playful and promiscuous, with asexual anatomies, like smiles without cats.

In the nomographic imagination, this bundle of tensions is linked to an emotional structure in which the masculinized emotions are interlaced with their alternatives. The origin of this emotional disposition can be traced back to Senecan stoicism, which does not call for a renunciation of the affects, but rather a practice of tempering them: "I am consumed by a great passion for temperance." This tempering of the passions has offshoots in other forms of subject constitution, ranging from practices of ordering (Primo Levi calls the passion constitutive of creativity a *formal defect*) to efforts to resist communitarian pressures to take distance from heterodoxies (for Alberto Mira, these pressures lead to a *thirst for normality*), to renounce complexities in favor of what Berlant calls "*the sheer vitality of normativity*."[23] This strategic simplification is the only possible response to the modern feeling *par excellence*, a feeling that assails us all: anxiety. Anxiety is prompted by questions of identity, nationality, work, and subjectivity.

Do It Yourself: Taxonomy and Hierarchy

In political theory, the phrase "bourgeois rationalization" has led a long and prosperous life. The phrase names the technical divisions between different forms of labor, which are separated into specialized compartments, all of them airtight. This separation organizes all spaces of work, including the creative sector. In this context – in this sector that defines itself as anti-bourgeois

– forms of classification are developed that, although they are conceived in an alternative spirit, in fact repeat the protocols of analysis and the taxonomic habits proper to the academy, as well as the vulgarized versions of these habits circulated by the media.

This alternative rationality can be seen, in the first instance, in the territorial spirit that characterizes protest movements. Dividing the world between "us" and "them," between dear friends and sworn enemies, involves recourse to a logic that derives from religious sectarianism. Hence the need to distinguish between the orthodox and the counterfeit, between the classical work and the mannerist one, between master and disciple. This injunction can only be realized through the elaboration of taxonomies that require the use of technical language. This kind of specialized jargon is derived from a theory of the sublime that is updated in the aesthetics of shock, impact, and extremes, which draws on elements of avant-garde aesthetics. *It is not museum directors who canonize and legitimate subcultural movements. It is their own publics who do this, with the help of various others, including specialized publications and festivals, which perform various roles, one of them institutional.* When it is a matter of elaborating and explaining our own experience – for instance, the experience of listening to a record, going to a concert, or taking part in a movement – our first recourse is to the romantic ideal of the creator. The band is romanticized by its public, which circulates heroic anecdotes and generates demands for rigor and purity, forming a cult with its own rituals, relics, and fetishes.

The canon that is the discography is gradually created and redefined by the musical press, which uses analytical and hierarchical criteria for this purpose: taxonomies, distinctions between subgenres, the intertextual description of an artist's recordings, and lists of the best recordings of the year, the decade, and history. These canonizing procedures are academic both in their origin and in their rhetoric. These journalists, we could say, have *degrees in the underground*. If these procedures exist, if the media outlets that circulate them still have readers, this is not because a handful of obscure and badly paid journalists decide they should. It is instead because the majority of listeners use these criteria as a kind of compass with which to orient themselves in the ocean that is the music industry. The process of legitimation thus does not begin in the academy; it begins with a conversation at a concert venue, when two avid listeners start talking about their favorite bands, using these resources, competing with one another to see who knows more about these bands, and staking their identities on this sort of knowledge.

There is thus an analytic model that is already at work in the streets, a popular spirit of hierarchy, a sort of spontaneous taxonomizing tendency. "The speed of time passing" is nothing other than a *taxonomic vertigo*.[24] Hierarchies are not so much imposed like systems of taxation as they are used as systems of classification; they emerge in part because they suit those in power, but also because they allow the dispossessed to interpret the world around them with more lucidity. *A world without hierarchy is, from the cognitive point of view, an unreadable text, and the majority of people prefer the ability to read reality, if only obliquely, to being free.* In order to question this perceptual and pre-scriptive apparatus, it is often necessary to work in a museum or a university, or preferably in both places, and to be someone used to wielding the critical tools necessary to building an alternative history of subcultures.

Why Do They Call It "Sex" When They Mean "the Ethical Dimension of the Doctrine of Relation"?

Nomography and Personal Relations

– I believe in the personal bond as such, in the identitarian value of its public exhibition, and in its social engineering for the sake of creating communities. *Ora pro nobis.*

Such is the belief that organizes the life that we share under affective capitalism. According to this shared imaginary, the social bond as such constitutes a value, is an end in itself, without end. Meanwhile, the public display of the social bond shapes identity. The latter is shifting and mutable only inasmuch as relational apparatuses are renewed together with their biological and technological frameworks. Crafting communities

34

out of officialized and publicly displayed bonds – this is the horizon of existence. One more step for humankind, the transformation of *homo sapiens* into *homo sociabilis*.

We could call this conviction *the doctrine of relation*, and we could define this doctrine as a sort of lay superstition characterized by a mystification that valorizes the social tie and communitarian performativity, and that is excessively confident in the diplomatic powers of spoken language. This relational doctrine unfolds in three interconnected movements. Its fetishization of the bond *as* bond locates the ethics of personal relations at the center of political debate. All ethics are articulated in rules, and *the more relational the world becomes, the more rule-bound it seems to us to be.* Regulations are usually thought to be the formal structuring of ethics, but in fact they represent ethics in ruins: the set of principles that are left after the collapse of communitarian illusions. Just as the material terrain of capital has been filled with ruins of the present – incomplete buildings, urban projects left half-constructed, the cost and rubble of financialization's fictions – so, too, is its imaginary landscape a graveyard of regulations, reprimands, and promises of punishment, which sought to govern forms of relationship and proximity that are now as outmoded and obsolete as any other product made for exchange.

A dysfunctional relationship is a crime. Only this premise, firmly installed in the collective nomographic imagination, can explain the extraordinary transformation that the figure of the murderer has undergone. Stories about psycho killers no longer show us the mournful facts; they no longer belong to the genres of gore. Instead they have become critical studies of the affective relations between the criminal and those close to him or her, and they remind us of Bergman rather than Argento. But they do not seek to bring remote regions of the psyche to life. Instead, they show us counterexamples of lives full of functioning relationships. And if Thanatos plays a minor part, becomes a mere supporting character in the current regulatory scheme, the same applies to Eros.

Are You Sure I'm Normal?

Masters of Sex is a series about hospitals. Well, not quite, since the majority of its protagonists are as healthy as can be. The only ones who are unwell are the doctors. The action takes place between the late 1950s and the 1960s. It could be a period piece. But the history that the show recounts is not a matter of parliamentary negotiations, but rather one of genital imperatives; it is not made by the founding fathers, but rather by their underlings. The first season is set at Washington University of St. Louis, where Doctors Masters and Johnson began their research. So, this might be a series about campus life. But in this academy, it is the teachers who, correcting their own practices, do the learning. So much so that every unusual finding and every indecorous conclusion forces them, episode after episode, to redefine the field of knowledge in which they work. This field is, obviously, sexology, a discipline with an inescapable destiny: rushing forward.

Masters and Johnson (or Bill and Virginia, for viewers of the series) embody this destiny. Sexology, tied in its beginning stages to the sciences of the psyche, developed before criminology, and, heir to the religious practice of confession, started out as an ethology of exceptional cases, that is, of "pathologies." Its clinical literature is full of monsters and obscurities, a gothic novel peopled with all kinds of creatures. The greatest sexologists, starting with Havelock Ellis, understood the necessity of leaving this behind in order to gain access to the more respectable realm of medicine. To achieve this, it was necessary to be dispassionate and a bit impersonal. It was necessary to speak less with the cops and more with sociologists, to substitute the word "mania" for "desire," and to explain the reasons for this in the most lucid possible way, by pointing to a bodily reflex, a neurological response. The word "paraphilia" had to be erased and replaced with "practice." It was, finally, necessary to give up gothic narrative conventions and replace them with the codes of regionalist storytelling, including touches of local color. In this process, the key word was, and still is, *depathologizing*.

"Am I normal?" Bill and Virginia, who were not normal themselves, were nevertheless great and relentless depathologizers. They invented machines with which to gauge the intensity of orgasms. They perfected vibrators. They filled page after page with graphics illustrating the cycles of arousal, which could be shown in curved lines drawn on graph paper, forming the peaks and pinnacles of an irresistible sensuality. They also made specialists in classical philology happy by providing authoritative confirmation of the ancient claim made by Tiresias: that women have more fun. They understood that, in their field, relativism was a form of cultural critique, and that, as Eve Kosovsky Sedgwick would say years later, "For some people, it is important that sex be embedded in contexts resonant with meaning, narrative, and connectedness with other aspects of their life; for other people, it is important that they not be; to others it doesn't occur that they might be."[1]

The Postcoital Selfie and the End of History

The creators of the series imagine that the books written by this anomalous couple are the products of an unresolved sexual tension, or one only barely resolved in cheap hotels and hidden corners. The hotel room is sad because the machines in it don't work. There's only a minibar and a television; without the technological supports that would allow for the study and quantification of spasms, their encounters are all yoking, union, coitus. That last, ugly-sounding Latin word, heard for the first time by a child, lets him or her intuit that *that*, the thing that is meant to be Fun Itself, can also be the most spectacularly boring thing in the world, unless something more is added to sad pieces of flesh. No, Virginia and Bill didn't manage to solve the problem, but they defined it very well and contributed to the effort to create a basis on which we might know what it is we talk about when we talk about Sex. Because above all what's needed is talk, which is more decisive than practice. We have all become observers, analysts, and commentators on sexuality. We have all developed a technical, documentary perspective on matters of the bed. We are all voyeurs, all anthropologists. We get between the sheets equipped with adult toys: a notebook, an analog imagination, and finally a cell phone with which to share our aftersex selfies. Those minutes of writhing, that homemade (or hotel-made) Kama Sutra: what is all this if not the prelude to a selfie? A self-portrait of the lovers at rest, with their half-smiles, "ruined by their delightful games,"[2] the selfie stick a penile elongation or feminine phallus, that emoticon grimace that lets us glimpse satisfaction or failure – what is all of this but another case in the global iconography of the postcoital? The digital photograph is not a unique image; it is not the "decisive moment" that the striving photojournalist once sought, but rather just one tile in a changing, transcontinental mosaic, made up of difference and repetition, that constitutes the typology of "after sex," the collective study of the vast expanse of beds, the continuity of cushions: a single, discontinuous thalamus.

After sex, ZTE: the Chinese smartphone or the seminal Samsung, with its South Korean technology, now embodies Otherness between the sheets. The Other to whom we open ourselves during sex, the Other who absorbs, penetrates, or rubs up against us, is no longer our companion in matters of love, but rather the camera, which sharpens focus, invades the bedroom, creates the scene to be represented, and, when its images circulate, generates myriad records of love's consummation. *To know* in the biblical sense thus becomes a form of *(self-)recognition* in the global mirror made up of those who proclaim *we did it, and* – there's precious little narcissism in this – *to be honest, it wasn't that great.* A collective dream pulsates in this plethora of interchangeable images, a dream that is shared in every bedroom and on every mattress, a dream of individuality, of dual identity, and thus a firm belief in the force of the event and the truth of the instant. But when we broaden the focus to consider how, say, on an Instagram profile, dozens of similar portraits are gathered, we can see that the self, whether individual or coupled, has been diluted under the semiotic regime of the web. The genre of the portrait, which used to aspire to show the *imago* of a peerless character or of a unique complicity, has lost the contest that had always pitted it, since its beginnings, against another genre: that of the snapshot defined as a "case" to be archived, whether by doctors or police. From the studies of facial morphology devised by the phrenologists to the recently developed uses to which this infamous science is put in airports, where images of passengers are generated in an effort to identify the terrorist, the trafficker, and the mule in the crowd's passage through metal detectors.

Bill's neurotic self-restraint has become the code that governs a more current masculinity; Virginia's pure energy is the model of an emergent femininity. When we watch as, attentive and distressed, they observe and record a patient's responses to stimuli, we see *sex becoming a form of work, the most private drives becoming "official," and pleasure becoming business, or otium, negotium.* We see, moreover, that it takes three to construct a couple: two who watch and a third who turns them on.

The Potentials of the Flesh

To correct not just the actualities but the very virtualies of behavior is the aim of modern legalism.[3] This goal stands achieved in the global panopticon that is the internet. Already for some time now, we have stopped using the phrase *digital reality* to refer to digital phenomena, because in the operations of social networks the adjective has been substantivized. The movements of web surfers are still, strictly speaking, virtual, but doesn't this virtuality have more substance and more coagulated fixity than our interventions in the analog world? This leads to a type of preventive and anticipatory vigilance in which the world imagined in Philip K. Dick's short story "The Minority Report" has been *realized*. Consider the officer who polices future crimes, the sleuth who investigates what has not yet happened but is yet to come, the internet user who catches people in the act of committing crimes of thought – since thinking aloud is the communicative principle of digital sociability – and denounces these sins before they become sins of commission. That is, assuming that the two types of sins are not already entirely overlapping, so that whoever thinks commits a crime.

Among the virtual sins that generate most interest – more than the organized banditry of the dark web – are those that insinuate, prefigure, or give us to understand what a body can do. Whether this is called *fleshly potential* or *sexual capital*, this possibility, latent in the body – when this body is shown semi-nude, suggestive, in the intermittent style of the softcore porn that every social network permits – is an object of scrutiny, not because of what it does but because of what it shows itself to be capable of doing. Vigilance: with a furrowed brow, a suspicious adult beholds the flowering of an adolescent. Don't grow up so quickly, don't develop breasts, don't stop being a little girl. The potential of the flesh acquires greater intensity when it is shown in a self-portrait, because this is the most decisive shift in perspective that digital photography allows for. It was only a very short time ago that we began to see images of naked female bodies, giving an account of themselves. Until the rise of mobile phones with cameras, the scenography of the nude, since its origins in sculpture, was organized by the asymmetrical relationship between the artist and his model. This gave rise to an aestheticized masculine gaze, projected onto a femininity that was eroticized in ways that were in keeping with the conventions of marble, oil, or the pixel. All of these conventions had something to do with the woman, but only very vaguely; they were really about the burning shade of femininity, its reflection in a golden eye.

But the status of pornography has also changed. Who would want to wear out his eyes watching videos of predictable sex acts, routine blowjobs – when he can see and record the guilty party *in flagrante*? The collapse of the porn industry, the amateur drift of the genre, and its feminization have all recodified the erotic image, made it into one more form of self-portraiture. At the same time, they have led to a discrediting of *the truth of sexuality*. Nude is the new clothed, and hidden truths, dirty Freudian secrets, must be sought in other expressions of this power.

Be Courteous, Please, or I'll Smash Your Face In

"I start a solitary game that involves insolently pawing at the couples who haven't joined in yet. They give me dirty looks that almost shatter my fantasy. Maybe I'm unknowingly breaking some swinger rule."[4] These sentences are taken from a series of *Sexographies*, in which the Peruvian author Gabriela Wiener chronicles the first visit that that she and her husband, the poet Jaime Rodríguez, make to "Swingerland." As in Wiener's other writings on subcultural communities defined by their uses of intimacy, the emphasis here is not on the flesh, but rather on the codes that regulate micro-social interactions. During the swingers' evening, some gestures are conventional, others unacceptable. The newcomer awaits assimilation into this regulated collectivity; she does not expect to penetrate it or be welcomed immediately.

This is a recurring trope in literary treatments of other forms of intimacy – in this case, more populous forms – and it could be defined as *the discovery of courtesy, or even courtliness, in liberal spaces*. We find a similar scene in Harold Jaffe's

46

fiction, in a passage in which he describes a first foray into a place called "the house of pain." Here the rules of health are different from those in force in the streets: "When Skag viewed me he said: 'I love your abs.' 'I love,' I said, 'your two dicks and faux puss.' He seemed to falter at the word 'faux,' but recovered and laughed a disarmingly high-pitched laugh."[5]

The genitality of the norm and the normativity of the genitals. Dissidence in matters of libido no longer involves singular moments of individuation; it has become a micro-social process of integration. The revolution celebrated by Wilhelm Reich is not a path from repressive community to emancipated subjectivity, but rather a parabola in which one set of cold rules of conduct is replaced by another, hot set for hot sex. An extended collectivity is abandoned in favor of a local agency, and a diffuse conventionality is overcome, but at the cost of compliance with a new courtesy. This new courtesy is more specific than earlier forms, since the more peculiar a collectivity is, the more "outsider" its status, the more clear and necessary is the set of rules that sets it apart.

No One's Style

You dress just like anyone else.

Your wardrobe is made up of the remnants of Inditex collections and clothes made by the brands that imitate Inditex. The jacket that you wear was almost trending in lawyers' offices and in government ministries during the Spring–Summer 2013 season. It's a corporate monkey costume that wouldn't be out of place at a Carnival celebration, because it would have been worn at the white-collar spring parties of the recent past, which is now the stuff of archeology, an ancient history more remote than Methuselah. And you won't be out of style even if you walk around on tiptoes in your practical Sebago shoes, because you don't even know the names of the magazines that govern fashion, the wellsprings that nourish novelty. When you see these on the newsstand, you confuse them with music magazines, and think of that past of yours . . . Although, if you stop to think about it, this strange anachronism that is your wardrobe, approved of by your aunts, your grandmothers, and airport security guards, is not as simple as it may seem. They wouldn't accept it in the collection at the Palais Galliera, the Musée de la Mode, because, look, they only *almost* manage to recreate the witty, bureaucratic style of six years ago: the man in his late fifties wearing a Venezuelan shirt underneath an Armani jacket. During his last haircut, this man asked, in the same voice that he used to complete transactions and finalize agreements with Deutsche Bank, for the barber to make dreadlocks out of those last remnants of hair still left on his shiny bald head, behind his ears.

Six years ago: this is the formula that Cory Arcangel devised to select the obsolete technological media out of which to build his successful works. This was a great discovery, a perfect voyage in a time machine. If they were made of junk that was up to five years old, they would be nothing more than the ruins of technological progress; if his sculptures used a color palette that resembled that of Microsoft Paint in its early days, which were now five years ago, they would not even be of interest to historians of internet art. But by delaying the machine, taking it back to an intermediate point, five-plus-one years in the past, He, the Archangel of History, with its planned obsolescence, managed to ride the winds of time into the future, achieving a style that is not worn out but rather retro, at once erudite and deliciously passé. In this way, he defined a chronological norm for the treatment of technological objects and the ephemeral aesthetics that they generate.

But you didn't know anything about this and didn't care to know anything about it, because, as you often say to your partner: "I don't understand all this modern stuff." To which she responds: "Well, look, I insist on going clothes shopping at Pull & Bear."

You wouldn't swear to it, but it seems that that absent-mindedness of yours, so healthy, hasn't prevented you from acquiring, by chance, the same habit as Arcangel, the artist who, despite his name and his singularity, is not a genius,

Cristóbal Fortúnez, *Fauna mongola*, 2010.

since there are none of those left. You are only someone who happens to have captured a key feature of the spirit of the age and of the Spirit of Digital History. This old age that you are squandering, this warmed-over look of yours, is, as the fashion magazines say of trends, *so out of style it's in!* You have positioned yourself so far from the fashion system, with its compulsively running machinery, that, without caring to and even unwittingly, you have ended up laying down its laws. And when those who subscribe to fashion magazines pass you on the street – they're on their way to this or that fashion hub, you're on your way to the Purgatory of office buildings – they look at you with surprise, with an envious is-he-or-isn't-he. They can't believe that you dress that way *in all seriousness*; they think your outfit is a calculated combination of vintage garments and accessories, a knowing mixture meant to produce or to simulate a sense of performative, ironic impersonality. In vain will you tell these people, again, what you tell your wife: these words, too, will be *so uncool they're cool*, and you will inspire imitators, incite passions. By the end of the night, you'll be in a small, pull-down bed in an apartment full of students, one of whom is an aspiring it girl who says she's nineteen. She'll tell you this just in time, and enjoy! But if I were you, I'd ask to see her ID before going any further. These days you never know.

On the other hand, you are dead, and so is the would-be it girl. You make up the perfect image of Susana and the Elders, Fashion and Death, because fashion is born dead: when a dazzling new collection appears on the runway, quite a bit of time already has passed since the designer completed work on it. She barely remembers what she did; she wouldn't even be able to recreate the patterns anymore, because her job forces her to work on coming collections more than a year in advance. And so now she's only thinking about the sketches for the season to come, when a model will shine bright in an outfit wholly inspired, from its contour to its colors, by your own image, by your daily fashion fare, by that awkward ensemble that is the cilantro and wasabi of the world of fashion. Thus what is sampled this season will be killed off by the anticipation of the following year, only to then be resuscitated six years later by the archangel . . .

And you are the arbiter of elegance.

On Cowardice

ALBERT: Do get *La Vie Parisienne*. [Unlike *Vanity Fair*] it's so defiantly normal!

> Noël Coward, *Semi-Monde* (1926, first performed in 1977)[1]

AMANDA: I think very few people are completely normal really, deep down in their private lives. It all depends on a combination of circumstances. If all the various cosmic thingummies fuse at the same moment, and the right spark is struck, there's no knowing what one mightn't do.

> Noël Coward, *Private Lives* (1930)[2]

Capital C Cowardice: a poetics of personal style developed in the plays of the English dramaturge and dandy Noël Coward. This Cowardice is made up of a way of dressing and a way of relating to one's own image, both based on two simultaneously held convictions. On the one hand, in the small worlds where fashion is highly prized and styles are fought over – where extravagance reigns supreme – when a *normality effect* suddenly emerges, a look inspired by common clothes, which do not seem to belong in this context, this generates surprise and leads, moreover, to the attribution of individuality and character to those who wear such clothes. On the other hand, despite appearances, in public life, the existence of a majority, or of the normal personality, is rare: these are mere suppositions or abusive generalizations that allow for the identification and description of singularities. In both cases, the normal is an exception: conspicuous for dandies, imperceptible for other, common people. In this way, the normal is suspended, caught between two oxymorons: it constitutes at once a *challenge* and a *minority*. Hence the will to dress in an anodyne way should be understood as a style in its own right, and not as following from a lack of originality. These are cases of Cowardice, not mere cowardice.

"I want to sleep with common people like you."

This way of *becoming a subject*, with its origins in the array of styles of the 1920s, marks the limits of fashion as a system of changes and permutations that favor originality. It opens the way to the aesthetics of the common that will be crystallized a century later in the movement known as *normcore.* Which has always existed, and existed long before it was codified as a style.

The Arbiter of Elegance and the Video Assistant Referee

Half-unzipped polar jackets. Texan clothes. Sweatshirts in solid colors. Giant sneakers without logos. Polo shirts with big lapels and two buttons. Haircuts from barbers who don't know that three-color lollipops are retro accessories. Bottles of Evian. And that casual and good-humored air that's so striking there should be a neologism invented to name it: not "simple" or "modest," but rather "unpresumptuous."

It was in 2013 that this unforeseen displacement from the opacity of fashion to the most common styles began to be seen.[3] In the game that has been played since 1858, when Charles Frederick Worth invented the profession of the designer, always pitting the special people against the common people, the arbiter of elegance stopped the clock, consulted the video replay, and to everyone's surprise awarded a penalty kick to the team with the *least* elaborate uniform. In the contrast between the standard and

Amina Bouajila, Illustration for *Elephant*, n°35, Summer 2018 (detail). In this still life gathering objects associated with alternative cultures, the Evian bottle, a normcore icon, on the left side of the image, figures as one fetish among many. The water that spills out from the bottle has left the mainstream and now forms a small tributary; the normal has been recast, made over to become a singular style and minoritarian passion.

the other, the latter was forgotten and the former declared glamorous, in an act of Cowardice. This movement inverted the distinctive operations of the fashion industry: rather than emanating from above, this look moved from the bottom up (inspired by some habits that had become conventions in Brooklyn). The primacy of the female body as a breeding ground for experimentation was replaced in a masculinization of fashion (where the "masculine" is defined by its "not stopping to think about what the hell it's wearing"). If, as I have indicated, the norm seeks to resolve chaos, then it should not surprise us that normcore would compete in, and win, the game of fashion, practicing a version of what's called *chaos magic*, a youthful form of psychedelia.

Fashion has always involved both differentiation and equalization, both the will to stand out and the impulse to blend in with the crowd. Georg Simmel identified this dynamic in his interpretation of obedience to the norms of fashion and the decision to conform, in one's personal behavior, to "a given example." This, for Simmel, can become a way of creating a façade, granting the subject an outward, visible conventionality, and thus of preserving, with this "veil and protection," the true, inner personality. This dynamic in turn generates a "conscious neglect of fashion."[4] Normcore is the most patent manifestation of this "conscious neglect," and at the same time it reveals the deep structure of the changes and developments of clothing.

What might have seemed to be a fleeting tendency was consolidated as an invariant in the social dress code, because normcore cannot be reduced to the materiality of a wardrobe. In order to define it, we need to refer to the most abstract feature of fashion: it is a relation of opposition and contrast between style and context. Designers and commentators took this basic structure and filled it, but with what? *With whatever* – that is, not with clothes that were carelessly chosen, but rather with those that could best represent *the whatever*. Repeating the Duchampian gesture that inaugurated twentieth-century aesthetics – the gesture that brought the vulgar object *par excellence*, the urinal, into the museum – and doing so in an age when the street had become a runway, Gvasalia and other designers took the unusual step of letting the image of *just anyone*, of any girl on the street, into their fashion shows. This was in fact an image and not the girl herself, in the same way that the Duchampian urinal was displayed not so that it might offer spectators the chance to relieve themselves, but rather to represent the object that could be exchanged for any other.

Normcore can likewise be understood as the systematic development of a performative logic according to which the anodyne isn't simply there but rather *appears*. It does not point to a deficit of sophistication, then, but rather represents a powerful entrance onto the scene. The fashion industry has, as always, staged this entrance most vividly: at the end of a lavish show, replete with walking costumes and unwearable clothes, the designer appears, smiling, greeted by a round of applause. This designer wears cowboy boots and a t-shirt. He is the only person in the room who dresses in this way, in just any way, and the applause recognizes both the originality of his creations and the irruption of the norm, of normal clothing, on the scene. In the great tradition of the dandy, this is an acceptance of the norm that only serves to negate it more.[5]

The same can be said of DJs. Anyone who goes to hear Fatboy Slim, Dan Deacon, or Dan Friel spin does not do this because she's attracted by the DJ's image. On the contrary, she does this very much *despite* this image. The distinctive experience of these shows is bearing witness to a radiant disconnect between the DJ's body and his work, seeing how a vulgar-looking guy, much less put together than his assistants, can nevertheless cause collective exaltation. It is a Dionysian experience, brought about by an Apollonian figure.

Normcore at once fulfilled the requirements of the Duchampian norm and updated this norm for the present, and it did so more cannily than many of the crypto-conceptual artistic practices that merely reiterate and glorify Duchamp's inaugural *urinary gesture*. Bringing the fine arts – which abandoned beauty after that first gesture – into contact with the applied arts – which stopped being decorative and became coextensive with life – the designers of *no one's style* took up their scissors and cut the Gordian knot of aesthetics, refusing the two principles of the fashion industry.

Anodyne? Divine!

The search for authenticity was finally abandoned. It was replaced by an effect caused by the *epiphany of the standard*. At the same time, the difference factory brought its machines to a halt, and designers defied the ban on the identical, on the equalized.[6] Thus, in the pages of *Vice*, the looks of bureaucrats and secretaries were declared dos; those of fashion victims, don'ts. And the people's *habitus* acquired the glamor of Armani and the gravitas of Bulgari, since it was now not only the most common culture; it had been recast as a subculture.

– And you, kid, what do you want to be when you grow up?

– W-when I grow up I want to be – I want . . . to be a sociological statistic and to appear with some regularity.

Desigual, or Difference

The opposition between normcore and chaos magic can be mapped onto the two sides in the battle between the fashion norms globalized by the Inditex Group and the lively "resistance" represented by Desigual, a brand that, according to its director, sells "not clothes but emotions." "Chaos magic" is a phrase that could surely be used to describe the company as well as the brand by which it was inspired and which it copied opportunistically: Custo Barcelona.

The company logos have been modified periodically to reflect current understandings of gender, so that the company's "evolution" is made to coincide with society's.

	Peret (1986)	*design*	Carlos Rolando (2011)
OUTLINE	ink		watercolor
COLOR	black		warm, watered down
STYLE	primitivist		psychedelic
TEXTURE	rigid		fluid
MATERIALITY	genital		discursive
FOUNDATION	biologistic		cultural
PHILOSOPHY	essentialist		constructivist
STRUCTURE	binary		ambivalent
NOMOGRAPHY	hetero		queer
HORIZON	hyper- (masculine – feminine)		a- or post- (gender)

"The spiritual meaning of the sexes, apart from their use in lascivious allegories, is their status as norms."[1] In this way, we could capture the traditional belief in the opposition between man and woman, understood as the primordial structure of the social order. Very different authorities have joined forces during the course of millennia to consolidate and reaffirm this binarism, which to many people still seems written in the stars, as if the bodies to which the words "man" and "woman" referred weren't carnal but rather celestial. But these are, in fact, anatomical and discursive ideals. All bodies aspire to them. But no one will successfully embody them.[2] To see this, it is not necessary to refer to pre-democratic regimes or to trace out all the ways in which intimacy is regulated in social-democratic life. This fundamental nomography, this feature of norms, is also present in the freest movements; it informs the operation and the writing of norms even at their most modern and progressive.

Design: drawing, tracing, taking shape in an outline, on the drafting table, in the studio, *designing oneself.* Peret's logo indexes the heteronormative schema that prevailed in the period of its design. It suggests – declares – how all Eves had to be at that time, with their Adams.

By contrast, Rolando's logo corresponds to another phase in the distribution of difference. Here Desigual no longer draws or retraces the primitive rule of binarism; nor does it dispense with the lascivious allegories of sex. It makes these, on the contrary, into fearless allegories, as in a television ad in which a delighted girl pokes holes in condoms. "Fluid" is the word of the moment, and the relationship between genders is thus represented by a joyous patchwork of watercolors, a *tutti frutti* of affective and sensuous flows, a lattice of floating, suspended bridges leading to sexual curiosity. Adventurers in self-design cross these bridges while dancing under a smiling Disney sun. The watercolor is a simplistic form of abstraction, and more specifically of a mode of abstract painting that might be called both *sexed* and *bimorphous*, which incorporates non-figural representations of the genitals into the visual field. The design's oldest antecedent is in this sense Jackson Pollock's oil painting *Male and Female* (1942). Among more recent painterly precedents, we can point to the work of Sue Williams. No more Eves and Adams, with their respective genitals; here instead we find unisex t-shirts and pants, primary bisexuality, polysensuality, a post-gender Benetton. In a word: joy.

In this case, we shouldn't speak of "sexes" but rather of "genders" understood as moments in and variations on the History of the Production of Biopolitics. The design unfolds in a moment that wears the dress of our friend Freedom. Desigual has made the epistemological shift that began at the turn of the century its very own, adding to this shift a vivacity that is often missing from its theoretical formulations. Desigual accepts Judith Butler's understanding of gender as a norm that can never be fully internalized.[3] But this impossibility is not, as in Butler, a source of anxiety, or, as in the work of Jack Halberstam, a constitutive failure. It is instead a matter of a mere typo or mistake. To commit this kind of error is not to fall victim to an ineluctable rule; it is to see oneself as a spirited, good-natured little creature, like a cartoon character. To attempt to conform physically to the law of gender is always to commit some kind of error. And each sexual orientation has its own corresponding narrative genre. The heterosexual failure to incorporate the norm is a light comedy, with moments of slapstick and touches of local color; by contrast, the gay version of this failure has traditionally been seen as a painful melodrama. The comedy can be a musical, with catchy numbers and memorable lyrics:

– Oops, I did it again! Again, I got the Law of Gender wrong!

– Haha, I guess you're just a fuckup, then.

– Ha, look who's talking.

Sexual difference doesn't matter. Desigual hath spoken.

The fashion system has always sheltered the ability to alter binarisms, to move the barrier that identifies, by separating, differences. This ability was already expressed in the name of the brand, with its semantic shift from the notion of gender *inequality* (in Spanish *desigualdad*) to that of bodily *anti-homogeneity*. The ability to alter binarisms is thus signaled by the s that, in the brand name, is inverted, becoming a z in its signage, in a move reminiscent of the Derridean concept of *différance*, here recast as an assertion of the value of differing as such, of the act or process of variation that distinguishes material forms from ideas. Nothing should surprise us about this translation from philosophy into fashion: the latter has always been a physics and metaphysics of corpo-reality, and there has always been a correlation between the two, all the more so now that the thought of *différance* has entered the market. This thought has become the principle that regulates the working of novelty, understood as an infinite series of singularities that acquire value by virtue of their external appearance of *differing* from one another rather than by virtue of their intrinsic properties.

The regime of *différance* that Desigual proposes is of course not exclusive to this company. Beyond its corporate politics, it presents itself as a sort of alternative order, a joyous hetero-doxy with its source in the fashion industry, that self-proclaimed vanguard of emancipatory ideals. The embrace of this kind of heterodoxy is contrasted with the company's own past, represented by Peret's logo, as well as with the approaches of its competitors. It is not difficult for Desigual to cast itself as the alternative to a principle of homogeneity. On every street and in any commercial district, its stores, lit by char-acteristic low-intensity bulbs, stand as the spatial realization of Desigual's psychedelic apparatus. Difference is luminous, sparkling. Such a store stands out all the more given its proximity to a Zara store, located a few steps beyond or across the street. Zara's crystalline sobriety at the level of both architecture and interior design looks severe compared to Desigual. The contrast between the normative order of a fashion universalized by Inditex and the lively "resistance" represented by Desigual is thus, *mutatis mutandis*, the national equivalent of the opposition between normcore and chaos magic.

Avant-garde when it comes to both gender and the Law: the code of legislation is continuous with the recodifications and counter-codifications of sexuality, and this continuity is made clear in the logo designed in 2011. The design serves as the perfect illustration of one of the most important juridical proposals to have been adopted on the terrain of biopolitics. I am referring to Article 12 of the Council of Europe Istanbul Convention, signed the same year, which obligates member countries to "promote [the] changes" necessary for "the eradication of prejudices, customs, traditions, and other practices which are based on the idea of the inferiority of women or on stereotyped gender roles."[4] Despite its generic and voluntarist nature, this proposal was met with predictable conservative responses, which denounced its effort to promulgate, from above, a new libidinal order in which heterodox minorities, thanks to the combined efforts of sophistic sodomites, gender-traitorous women, and diabolical lawyers, would, heaven forbid, lord it over the healthy and procreative sexual majority.[5]

Desigual's drift recalls the movements made by other alternative organizations. The grunge band Nirvana engaged, throughout its brief career, in a comparable drift. First there was the album whose celebrated cover shows a baby swimming, with small but unambiguous genitals. Cobain and his bandmates established themselves as an alternative to metal, which by the early eighties had entered the kind of mannerist and repetitive phase that announces the end of a musical style. Then, in their songs, lyrics like "everyone is gay" were clearly addressed to a more diverse community than the one made up of metalheads, who had always imagined themselves as macho, as hyper-masculine.

– Gender? *Nevermind!*

In this way, a permissive norm is established, a shared structure of originality that gathers, or shelters, the unclassifiable and the exceptional. But what is the status of this exception, and how is it related to the great tradition that *respects* the barrier that separates the genders? The first response is the one most suited to corporate rebranding strategies, and it is as follows: the intrinsic liberalism of "alternative" market sectors has been recognized and espoused, in an act of voluntarist good faith, by the masses. By this account, the masses would have accepted the idea that binary distinctions are now History, the notion that the schooling in gender that we all received is now obsolete, and the countervailing claim that the open-ended formula "LGBTQI+" has been broadened to include even the "H" for "hetero." There would be no more hetero identity, then, but instead a plurality of hetero acts and hetero performativities, defined by their opposition to the norm they violate and their proximity to and sympathy with other practices. These are no longer located on the other side of a barrier, but rather right here; they are available as resources, possibilities, tools. There will be no more "opposite sexes" or "equal loves," because no identity will be defined by oppositions or trade-offs. No one's sexual profile is identical to anyone else's, or even identical to itself. Such profiles cannot be captured by the names of stable orientations. At the same time, the idea of *sexuality* itself, formerly thought to follow from or fall short of genitality, has been diluted, like watercolor pigment; it now forms part of the less anatomical, the more diffuse and sentimental, concept of *affect*.

Welcome, then, to the Promised Land of divergent, *desigual* affects.

According to this affirmative reading, Desigual no longer advertises dresses and shirts. It delivers instead an Annunciation that is messianic. In a self-fulfilling prophecy, Desigual promises the advent of a society long-awaited by progressives. This is a gender politics that will be acceptable at both ends of the political spectrum. It will fulfill the evolutionary desires of the left and at the same time seek to assuage the fears of those on the right by presenting change as something serene, a process guided not by revolutionary fervor, but rather by a kind of liveliness, a tenderness shot through with the banal colors of conservative affect.

But if it is differences that we are talking about, then there is always something that comes between the fictions of advertising and the reality in which they seek to intervene. This is the utopian dimension of the nomographic imagination. It is "utopian," because the place where it takes place, its *topos*, is the space of advertising, understood as a sort of externalized unconscious. By contrast, in the material realms where everyday difference is negotiated – the difference that Desigual, in a faint echo of deconstruction and queer theory, wants to have overcome – the exceptional has a very different nature.

In the opposition between the normal and the pathological,

> It is not just the exception which proves the rule as rule; it is the infraction which provides it with the occasion to be a rule by making rules. In this sense, the infraction is not the origin of the rule but the origin of regulation. It is in the nature of the normative that its beginning lies in its infractions.[6]

The models featured in Desigual's advertisements, jumping and exchanging smiles, are never anomalous; if they are exceptional, this is only because of their beauty, not because they embody an unprecedented relation to gender. A very beautiful model on whose skin we can see the signs of vitiligo is not, a priori, a queer subject.

The fictions of advertising show us *a stylization of hetero beauty*, not a difference with respect to the hetero norm. When it comes to clothes, these don't in any way resemble the post-gender designs developed by companies like Army of Me, or the a-gender fashions of La Haine. To dress up as a hetero woman wearing multi-colored clothes is not to take a step outside the norm; it is, rather, to add some elements from an infantile wardrobe, some others that look like the umpteenth corporate version of hippy style – but not, of course, hippy style in the sense of counter-culture, but rather *a hippyish look* – and others that we could in good faith call *freakish* and that summon the spirit of '68. More specifically, of May 6, 1868, the day when the Hungarian poet Karl Maria Kertenby wrote the letter in which the words "homosexual" and "heterosexual" appear for the first time.[7]

To dress heteros in a queer-friendly way, to play at hetero anomaly in order to then reinscribe the norm, to add a silent H to an acronym: this, in fact, is the world promised by Desigual. Here we see an idea at work that is very typical of heteronormative thought, in which a plurality of experiences and attitudes that do not adhere to the rules are assigned to the confused category of "the gay," treated, for its part, as though it were a synonym of "the unregulated." This is a mobile idea that presupposes that desire can be defined as the norm's preference for itself, and a longing for freedom on the part of those who do not behave in bed the way one does oneself. But it is worth asking: what is this freedom that one so chivalrously renounces, in order to give it to someone else? These are strange liberators indeed, given that this idea of "the gay" has only been used for one thing: to try desperately to broaden and shore up the "the middle class" at a historical moment when it is impossible to keep believing in its existence – unless, of course, the acts and attitudes of some gay people who belong to this class are taken to be representative of a collective identity defined by sexual orientation. So, yes: the realm of the middle class, impoverished by systemic crises, undermined by the omnipresence of the culture industries and their increasing segmentation, is lit up and suddenly appears as a *locus amoenus* or safe space, a place for everyone – yes, even for you people!

From this perspective, the comparison between the two logos carries a different meaning. There is a historical difference between these two logos, but the consequences of this difference are much more profound than the second logo seems to suggest. Precisely because the "promissory" logo designed by Ronaldo is abstract – just as the idea of a post-gender *paideia* is still an abstraction, formulated but not realized, a future horizon or destiny for fashion – it only conveys meaning by projecting itself onto, or covering over, the old logo. This old logo, although it has ceased to function as a corporate emblem, is still used as a retro point of reference in various designs. And, as in an oil painting by Pollock given the title *Male and Female*, it continues to form the material reality and the normative foundation with respect to which the exceptions and pseudo-anomalies – the curiosities – can be defined. Desigual's ad campaign thus isn't queer but rather *curious*, in the sense of being a variation on heteronormativity that, once in a while, sympathizes and colludes with deviations from the norm.

If the procedure that is proper to the decorative arts involves adding to Creation with external embellishment, then the New Order is defined by its *reconstitution of binary sexual difference as a retro art* – now that all works of art and all efforts at political intervention are retro – and its *decoration of this difference with the curiosities found outside gender norms*. The hetero norm, decorated, haloed in this way with rarities, is given an aura of the psychedelic; it becomes a matter of flow and sparkle; it updates itself and attains what the dominant culture seeks: a displacement of its image from the center of the iconosphere. This image is displaced in the collective imaginary, and the hetero norm then seems to be *just one subculture among others*, the bearer of all the modesty, prestige, and singularity that the subcultural always bears with it.

On the Norm Considered as One of the Fine Arts

Someone has caused a body – a body or two, a pair, a patriarch, a majorette, a wave – to enter a spasmodic state. Someone has caused this, or someone has pulled this off; we can't say which, because unleashing the force of spasms in a body, or bringing this body to a spasmodic state, is either the best thing you can do to it or the worst thing that can be imposed on it, the cruelest, the optimal, the most disastrous, the highest, a thorough dismantling of yourself, nerve by nerve, or an experience of the most intense sensation that you have ever felt. Carried into the air by this sensation, I managed to forget myself, to fall in a sequence of lessening convulsions that came, one after another, just after the other's, the reflexive movement, the muscular insistence, the arch of the neck and bridge of the back, the slow end of the round of convulsions, spaced out now, each time less intense and softer. And the body, which had been until just a minute ago much more than itself, beside itself, thrown out of orbit, seems now to return to its former state and to find itself again. It will soon be whole again, bony, anatomical, but not just yet: not until the moment when the last trembling muscle, still relaxing, speaks, has its say, not until it says the word: *convulsion*.

The convulsion of the hands, trembling in pure anger, and together with the hands the Tablets of the Law, grasped, trembling, the bosom of the patriarch, the flowing beard of the prophet who, just after his descent, without even time to catch his breath, sees, amid the shouting, amid the crowd, the Calf, the object of blasphemous adoration. And still holding, all atremble, the mystic Tablets, with a grimace of disgust on his face, he is seized by a feeling, greater than disappointment, redder than rage. And right there before the impious celebration he feels for the first time – he invents, without knowing it – biblical outrage, the height of sacred indignation, his flesh quaking and the marble convulsed. He's beside himself, beside God, and, moved by rage, he feels the iconoclastic impulse emerge, his forearms ready to throw the Tablets, break them, let them fall, seized by prophetic tremors. He already intuits that the material in his hands will be shattered, as will the letters, the commandments. And in time Moses will become Pete Townshend, destroying his guitar on the wooden planks of the stage, and all that's left is to clarify whether the breaking of the Tablets, that definitive moment of convulsion, is the opposite of orgasm or its complement. Shards from Sinai, dust of the Decalogue. Isn't another body indispensable for the achievement of orgasm, even if this body is merely the sinuous outline of the letter, the anatomy of the law, unraveled? But one thing is for sure – they are one and the same: the law is convulsed, and sex is normotic; calamity is sensual; orgasm, juridical.

The compulsion to regulate, orgasmic order, art, the word spoken by the last relaxing muscle.

Exodus 34:29: The Cheerleader Patriarch

Nomography is a regime of images and an apparatus that organizes aesthetic effects. I mean this last phrase in the sense in which it is used by Canguilhem, according to whom a logical norm, inverted, becomes an aesthetic norm.[1] This happens in the biblical episode in which Moses breaks the Tablets of Stone, which is also the story of an impossible repetition: the ridiculous and exemplary tale of a bearded man and his tablets. In Freud's celebrated study of Michelangelo's sculpture of Moses, the patriarch is the model of a "great man," implacable and irascible, although we are also asked to notice that our focus shifts when we see the sculpture: here the stress falls not on the protagonist himself, but rather on his tablets, and the fear that these will break assuages or inhibits Moses' anger. In Michelangelo's recasting of the biblical account, we see an example of a man "struggling successfully against an inward passion for the sake of a cause to which he has devoted himself."[2] The portrait of the outraged patriarch will be remade again by Nicolas Poussin, and then again in Richard Hamilton's *The Funhouse* (*This is Tomorrow!*) (1956), an emblem of the modern nomographic disposition.

The patriarch, guarantor of the Laws, is himself moved beyond the commandments. He becomes the first to exceed the order of these laws, in an originary misalignment between the divine letter and humankind. He is *exemplary* in that he demonstrates how the legal order, once installed, opens a void, *creates* crime, which it needs in order to be valid. As soon as the bearer of the legal order reached civilization, it became clear that the Ten Commandments were in fact incomplete. "Thou shalt not break the Tablets." "Thou shalt not excuse thyself by pointing to your compatriot's irresponsibility." These are the first two commandments that were missing. And this is the most important: "Thou shalt not ask God to remake what cannot be put back together." In violating this last commandment, Moses obliges God to repeat himself, to invent repetitive time despite himself. This gives rise to a Law that is not original, but rather a copy or an imitation, to Tablets that return in a kind of *dejà vu*, shards put back together, pieces of norms. Could this repetition of the Law be anything but hyperbole?[3] From this point on, it will be necessary to obey the breaking of the tablets; wherever we are, we will live with the consequences of this accident at once orthographic and epistemological, caught between the law and fury, between regulation and havoc, between the clear outlines of the sacred and the most graceless profanation.

Theories of masculinity have shown us that the figure of the patriarch is the representative of the phallic order *par excellence*. This order, developed aesthetically throughout the twentieth century, gives gender violence a cultural alibi.[4] The issue of gender norms – cultural, cinematic, Hollywood-inspired – is foregrounded by Hamilton, who in his collage updates the tale of the Golden Calf, replacing the painterly motif of ritual sacrifice with a photographic version of abjection. There are sodomites (the male couple, looking like they're in a Western), virile women (including a *femme fatale* from film noir, here shown grasping at the would-be masculine weapon), and orgies. This Moses, whom a can-can dancer seems to imitate with gusto, will not manage to melt down the Golden Calf, as happens in the scriptures. His presence, his hystericized masculinity, gathers the various elements of the collage together; without meaning to, he seems to coordinate, if not choreograph, the blasphemous dance in which the laws of gender are violated. In the sacred pantomime of the patriarch, we see an instantiation of the Derridean claim that "parody supposes a loss of consciousness, for were it to be absolutely calculated, it would become a confession or a law table."[5] It is "both regulated and without regulation: it must conserve the law and also destroy it or suspend it,"[6] as when the prophet raises his tablets above the impious and agitated pagan crowd.

Moses, beholding cinema's polytheism, raises his bare arms and flails, with his coat billowing. His pose is suggestive. He looks like a cheerleader. His is an inciting, animating law, and the patriarch, the son of Amram and Jochebed, prohibits the way a cheerleader cheers. Censoring, he riles up the crowd:

– Give me an L! Give me an A! Give me a W! *(All together!)* LAAAW!

She appears on the cover of *American Cheerleader* and *L'Osservatore romano*; today her uniform is a passionate red, and she's a puckish prophetess, ruler of my insides. But in concert she appears in the stadium wearing a pleated plaid miniskirt, light blue and white, smelling of divine pussy. She knows how to do a backbend without showing her underwear. She's bearded like a bear who's a bottom, and at dusk the hipster guys line up to suck her off.

The lead can't figure out what the movie's about. This is a scenario that seems to define Charlton Heston's acting career. A couple of years after *The Ten Commandments* (1956), during the filming of *Ben-Hur* (1959), he was the only person on the set not to know that the person he was playing was gay. In a scene between Ben-Hur and his arch-enemy Messala, who had in fact been his lover, the actor playing Messala, Stephen Boyd, deployed a kind of performative doublespeak, alternating between hypermasculine and hetero gestures of friendship and another set of gestures whose meaning remained unperceived by his scene partner.[7]

Go down, Moses! As in that classic spiritual, the patriarch went down, broke down. In his effort to transmit the law, he made it descend from the peaks of the ideal to the gutter of materiality. As in *The Funhouse*, artistic practice develops in an effort to adhere to the law but also eroticizes the law, and this prevents the subject's disparate practices from devolving into psychosis. If the legislator can ignore the implications of his legal acts and constitutional improvisations, subjectivity is likewise governed by what Butler calls "a paradoxically enabling set of grounding constraints."[8] The artist is enabled by the norm – not by refusing it, but by reproducing the paradox that the norm is. Art is not made up of a contest between the norm and its transgression, but rather is formed by a dynamic involving both imagined normativity and the norm of denormativization.

What is an Artist, and Why Does the Artist Always Seem to Ask for the Slaps Not Received in Childhood?

The artist is distinguished from all other mortals by a singular displacement in her way of perceiving responsibilities. These are always arranged along a scale from minor to major obligations: that is, from practices or acts that would be preferable to engage in, to those that one ought to engage in, to those that one must engage in. The name that we give to the first of these three sets of responsibilities is *conventions*; the second we call *norms*; the third, and most serious, *laws*. Anyone who hasn't been touched by the Muses knows that tipping in a restaurant is a convention, and that not wearing a skirt if you're a man is a norm. And such people do not kill others, because this is the law. In addition to knowing these things, most people *feel* them, and this makes it possible to perceive the variations and deviations that these figures of responsibility allow for. The artist also knows this, but because of the peculiar qualities of her work, which places her in a position that is intrinsically in conflict with responsibility (here defined as a functional tie to a creative tradition), she cannot act accordingly. She can't, because instead she perceives conventions as though they were norms and norms as though they were laws. And she perceives laws in the way Kafka's characters do, as if they were not the material results of the labor of jurists, but rather the emanations of a divine and negating Power. It is this power – and not the expressionism to which it often refers – that is, strictly speaking, Kafkaesque. For this reason, and not because of his shy reluctance to publish, the Czech writer is the model of the modern author; he offers the first account of the psychological experience of a diffuse and omnipresent law, inscribed in every skin and in every psyche. This diffusion gives rise to a heightened form of "correct perception" when it comes to our responsibilities, and of the reasons we are subject to them.

The word "problematic" suits the artist. This word in fact expresses the nature of the artist's relationship to responsibility, to the coercive dimension of life in a community. It is usually said – formerly in manifestos, nowadays in interviews, artists' statements, columns, and proclamations – that the artist finds Freedom in this problem and uses this freedom to create works of art. With these words, the artist elicits applause and affirmation from the public, which expects nothing less from her. And this is a good thing, since the artist's works would be completely without effect, significance, or ground if it weren't for the force or this founding problem. In and through this agreement, the public receives, in the act of consumption, a microdose of Freedom: a lay person's experience of sin, whether of thought, word, or, when the work of art is interactive, deed. But, oh, the creator does not participate in this experience, despite the lip service she pays to emancipation. In fact, Prometheus-like, she has been tied to a rock, punished for having betrayed the gods by giving away their fatuous fire. Here the romantic theory of the creative personality is correct: in fact, the artist gives up her freedom so that others may enjoy it in her place.

Many chains hold her captive. There are fetters that tie her to her editor, others that tie her to her publicist, her gallerist, her agent, and the media that have supported her. And there are of course the fetters that tie her to the public, which in turn demands more straps and cords: one for those who appreciate her art, another for those who want to value it, another for the spectator she imagines during the act of creation, who will never be in agreement with the real collective that is her fanbase. And since the rise of the meta-media – since the consumer of a work of art assumed the obligation to become a follower of its maker, who in turn follows him back lest she risk losing a potential client – each spectator bears a chain, each aficionado a padlock.

The strongest of these ties comes from the imperative to experience, day and night, a heightened, hyperbolic sense of responsibility, to show a greater degree of "correct perception," always with a supplement of intensity and anguish. It might be said that this situation is not the artist's alone, and that on social networks we can see, in all kinds of profiles and in a wide range of fields, that a structure is taking shape, a personality type and set of functional behaviors that are hyper-relational. And so it is: on Facebook and Twitter, the old dream of becoming an artist comes true for every living creature. But more tears are shed when prayers are heard than when they go unheard, and the result has not been what the vanguardist libertine program envisioned and longed for, that plethora of uncontained expressivity that would have broken straitjackets and burst through dams, unleashing riots in every prison and orgies in every office, leading us dancing toward the Brave New Genital World, our hips swaying to samba and our lips singing in chorus.

No fucking way. Following the path of the artist, now the average citizen and prosumer – like an artist in that he's "disturbed" or, more often, just a technologically addicted mess, putting on airs and making a garish spectacle of himself – has also been tied down, tied to others, defined by the singular displacement that lets him rise above his station, going from his pedestrian path to the Creator's pedestal. And, of course, these people have also given up their Freedom – the freedom that the singular artist once lent them, with her works, when it was still possible to distinguish between producers and consumers, between

Leonardos and commentators. But if this freedom has been given up, then who has taken it over?

No one. Now there is no one in a position to enjoy this freedom. The global determination to create freedom by means of art, universalized and by now unanimous, has rendered the old race of spectators – those today disdainfully called "passive" – extinct. They stand accused of social phobia, electoral abstention, the banal crime of being merely contemplative, melancholic. Hey, spectator, you lazy chancer, don't look at us. Join us! This call is the result of the aestheticization of the world, which does not consist in having replaced the pure signified with mere show, for this has been happening at least since the Parthenon was built. Instead the aestheticization of the world follows from the compulsive production of Freedom under the sign of the sacred norm of Displacement, to the benefit of No One. As Kafka might have put it, there is Freedom, but it's behind this door. It was open only for you. Now I am going to shut it.

What Is a "Provocation"?

"This work was made as a provocation." We often hear this claim made of certain works of art and in media responses to these works. The claim is made in a resigned tone, as though it were a matter of common sense. But according to Pedro Miguel Lucía, what we call "common sense" is a matter of advanced study. Common sense is also a synonym for "success": it represents the victory of an idea that has, in its trajectory, reached such a level of credibility that it no longer needs to be explained, because it has managed to eliminate all alternatives.

The claim "this work was made as a provocation" is based on four premises: (a) there is a general, shared criterion for responding to the issue that the work addresses, and a consensus on how this issue should be addressed; (b) the artist knows of this criterion and keeps it in mind while creating her work; (c) among the motivations that the artist had for creating the work – biographical, psychological, ethical, and so on – the main motivation must have been the call of common sense; and (d) among potential spectators – specialists, friends, future readers – the artist must perforce have chosen "the general public," a susceptible public, and addressed her work to it.

This fourfold prejudice – a prejudice that pre-judges and preempts the act of aesthetic reception – might be considered democratic. Too democratic, in fact! In the name of a social-democratic totalitarianism, the work's various potentialities have been reduced to an engagement in dialogue with an agreed-upon arch-reader, who then becomes a ghostly authority, because public opinion is not written in heaven. In order to invent it, you need a whole host of journalists, licensed to speculate.

Anyone who has experience in the art world knows that this imaginary model of "provocative communication" is only rarely operative, because the criteria used to determine a work's relevance are increasingly specific and have become difficult to explain to those without proficiency in the field in which the work intervenes. There are, however, isolated cases in England, for example, where a part of the scene is structured this way: there is a small theater full of artists who proclaim, "Pay attention! Because I'm about to touch a nerve." But this is an individual instance; it is not representative of the functioning of even this sector of the arts scene, and it is revealing that such an unusual phenomenon has been discussed in and disseminated by the media as though it were the order of the day.

And why would England, the country of Brexit, be the place that sets the tone for these debates? The choice is conjunctural, arbitrary, and melodramatic. What makes this nation the ideal place for "stimulating debate" is not that it is the home to any important biennial – if it were, then we would not need to look to Basel, Miami, or São Paulo – or that it is home to the critical literature – as are Berlin, Paris, and New York. It is instead the image, still vivid in the collective unconscious, of a civilization divided between two symbols: monarchic formality and lumpen punk rock. An island of aristocrats and hooligans where a carefully considered editorial published in *The Guardian* can come into conflict with another, hysterical one published in *The Sun*.

We can thus speak of the act of provocation as one of the dramatic arts. It's a kind of happening based on the presumption of collective participation, one in which the key protagonist is not the artist but the public. The former plays the role of sacrificial lamb, in keeping with a dramatic tradition that is traceable to the first stagings of the Passion and that extends to modern plays that explore the community as horde.[9] This is a normative happening, then, in which the principle of correction is announced not by the law-giver, who is merely a secondary character, but rather by the spontaneous collectivity, which becomes an indignant spectator. In the form of tweets, Facebook status updates, and all manner of other digital notifications, this spectator produces the norm that the work appears to have transgressed. The norm and the work thus trade places, exchange functions. In this normative happening or nomographic drama, the work is presented as a given, a finished product – and this despite the fact that contemporary creativity tends to prioritize the processual, the open, the improvisational, and other forms of trust that "God will provide," placing faith in the future or the course of time in what we might call a kind of *aesthetic providentialism*. By contrast, normativity, which seeks to be static and immovable, surges forth, flows. A collective emergence, it is at once outburst and Law, nominal and anonymous. It acquires ever more agency as later contributions are made, in real time.

Even quite recently, this kind of happening only took place of an evening in the cordoned-off spaces of the cultural sphere. So it was, or so it was said to be, in the media as they were understood during the twentieth century: those "independent" tabloids (which meant independent from rival corporations), those urgent rags, those sources of infotainment made by consulting the Elements of Style, those purveyors of alienation printed in color and three columns, those two-for-one deals at the newsstand. The transfer of information to the web, the redoubling of the media by the meta-media, in which each person has his or her own profile – and responds to the claim "we want to know your idiotic opinion" – gave rise to another metamorphosis. The passive reader became a source of opinion, susceptible and responsive, a pal and a commentator, a soloist speaking in tongues and ready from the first to raise hell over the most negligible news. The happening and provocation were moved from the culture supplement to the politics section, so much so that the debate over the minutiae of local politics became the new *Kultur*, the real communicative context and point of reference, as we can see in the online profiles of writers, who talk of nothing else. The Pantomime of Provocative News and the Hypersensitive Twitter User. This was how "provocation" stopped being a small matter of small disturbances in the news cycle and became the news itself, the current in which we are all dragged along like F. Scott Fitzgerald's "boats against the current," caught in a storm. Although we sense that this is not Jay Gatsby's destiny, we will not find catharsis in it either, because the tempest takes place in a teapot, and you and I have caused it, together with the rest of the internet. This collectivity might then be, depending on the level and the nature of the "provocation" in question, a horde, a kindergarten, a principality, a *mêlée*, a gang, or a phalanx. It might engage in enlightened gossip or sedentary hacktivism. But – although this claim may scandalize, I will not fool myself into thinking otherwise – it will never be a Community.

The Museum and the National Bureau of Norms

The whole world seems to agree with the inventor of outsider art when he tells us that "what we ask of the work of art is certainly not that it be normal. . . . Because in the end the individual who is normal in the official, state sense of that word works in his office or a factory, but it does not occur to him to make paintings."[10]

Nevertheless, during the years when these sentences were written, there were paintings that were not made for the purpose of being works of art. This was the case with *El aguafuerte perfecto* [*The Perfect Etching*], made collaboratively in 1970, by Luis Camnitzer, the founder of Uruguayan conceptualism, and the US architect Stephen Klein. "It was to be to other prints what the platinum meter in Paris used to be to other meters" throughout the world. The artist's offered this piece to various institutions. The National Bureau of Standards in Washington sent a gracious but negative reply "indicating that their standards were of a different nature."[11] By contrast, the head of collecting at the Whitney

Museum in New York responded without delay, saying: *bring it here.*

These are two models of the artist, then. The *outsider* integrates herself into the romantic tradition, which valorizes singularity over academic training, emphasizing the importance of psychic illness as a source of originality, and adding the occupants of asylums to the ranks of lay geniuses. At the other extreme, we find the *insider* (a virtual synonym of the "conceptual artist"), who has studied and learned all the principles that organize the art system, starting with its procedures of legitimation. He approaches this system as though it were a world unto itself. We can contrast the heterodox practice of the outsider, who paints or sculpts from a place outside the History of Art, with the insider, with his paradigmatic will, who conceives of no other history than that of Art, and whose work ceases to be *plastic* in order to become *discursive.* And discourse finds its privileged form in the paradigm: the work that elevates itself to the status of model, giving up authorial individuality to become instead a template, projected into the future.

Less popular than the outsider, this other figure, a strange sort of creator, embodies the

dehumanized principle that is the basis of all creative practices. She does so at the cost of going
beyond all subjective vision and giving herself over
to the impersonal impulse that, though sometimes hidden by the effusions of the inspired ego,
traversed the aesthetics of the twentieth century
to the point of taking it over. Being a machine.
Being No One. Being one of Columbus's ships
as advertised on television, becoming a stone lion
who contemplates the river that passes by. It is the
will to negate the ego that is found in styles like
geometric abstraction, where, as Xavier Rubert
de Ventós notes, "regularity is no longer found
in the heavens, as in the Middle Ages, but rather
in mechanistic laws. One can finally go back to
painting laws instead of things."[12]

This impersonal frame of mind has characterized various aesthetic achievements – so many, in
fact, that it might be considered an invariant, a
disease of impersonality that cancels out any kind
of individualist illusion. Boris Groys identifies
this force at work in installation art, where the
artist no longer proposes or suggests, but rather
installs himself as the legislator of an autonomous
space. "In fact, to be a paradox-object," he writes,
"is the normative requirement implicitly applied

to any contemporary artwork."[13] The etching, in other words, must be at once an invention and a product, at once poetic and technical.

There Is No Institution But You

In order to integrate yourself impersonally into the History of Art, you need to develop a peculiar approach to the institution. As the case of the etching shows – with its aspiration to the condition of a mere case, not the emanation of the artist's personality – the institution is addressed with profound ambivalence. The artist calls at its doors, asks for its approval, and, at the same time, pulls off a sophisticated trick with the aim of pointing to a blind spot in its politics of inclusion. It is because of this latter aspect of its work that this approach is called *institutional critique*. The term has, again, a Kafkan resonance. It makes us think of a very thin, very small person, on tiptoes, a weakling, hesitantly testing the doorknob on the giant door that leads to the Courts. Knockin' on Hell's Door.

But it is a misreading of Kafka's works that has informed the modern understanding of the *institution* in the collective imaginary, and that has led to its unpopularity, all the greater in the world of the Fine Arts. To read the most influential of Kafka's novels is to see, among other things, that an institutional entity, the judiciary, has the capacity to *dehumanize* anyone who falls prey to it. This accounts for the fact that the verb *dehumanize* has become synonymous with *institutionalize*. Nevertheless, to continue to read Kafka's works is to realize that a premodern profession like that of the country doctor also has the capacity to dehumanize its practitioner. And the same happens to the Traveler, to the slave who builds the Great Wall, and to the hunger artist. The lawyer – is he any more human than the servant? We thus see that dehumanization is not a historical phenomenon and is not the child of the Industrial Revolution or of Nazism. It is a narrative structure that leads to the dismantling of a character. This process is inherently comical, but its comedy is not gestural or situational. Kafka's humor instead follows from his exposure of the insubstantiality of the human, which can only be defined by referring to an ill-fated encounter with another form of Humanity, one that we only take to be more solid because it bears the name *institution*. Indeed, it institutes and institutes itself, while the poor human only substitutes him- or herself for, stands in for, supplants, the idea of Humanity. The human can thus only be defined in a retrospective fashion, in a moment of destruction, while it's blown to pieces. *Now that I see it toppled, I conjure up the qualities that defined it, after the fact.*

Dehumanization exists; the human does not. This is a necessary premise for the creative practice that I am describing. The creator as institutional critic proposes projects addressed to some public or private power, which allows for the unfolding of an irregular activity or consents to the use of its facilities for improper ends. As is to be expected, the plan cannot be carried out in the way it was envisioned, or it has to be substantially modified. But the unrealized initial project is not some kind of incomplete masterpiece. Nor is it a total failure. On the contrary. Because the objective, whether implicit or explicit, is not to acquire a definitive form, but rather to speak to the powerful, to discover norms or prompt the creation or improvisation of new norms to stand in the way of the work's realization. In this way, a farce is staged, with the artist-dreamer pitted against repressive authority:

– Go ahead, stand in my way, remind me of a prohibition! Please. And tell me why you're doing it.

A bird in search of a cage. . . . Institutional critique is an aesthetics of friction. It involves the chafing of the artist against authority, a collision that is sought out. What a disappointment if the artist fulfills her objective! Imagine being an avid reader of Kafka, compelled to go to an administrative office to renew your passport. You go expecting – hoping – to get your fill of sordid bureaucracy and existential grey, only to find – horror of horrors – a clean and well-lit room. So much light! People are taking numbers, and the electronic display showing these numbers works just fine. How could it work?! Franz, Franz, why have you forsaken me? And instead of waiting for two days, you only have to wait for twenty minutes to talk to a – monster? A creature from the abyss? Wait, no, this pen that the woman has in her hand – is that from the Tate Modern gift shop? What can you do, poor wretch, but get down on your knees and beg:

– Please! Don't do this to me! Tell me that I'm violating a policy! Smoke a Marlboro and send a cloud of smoke into my face while you file my application in the trash! Read *The Sun*! Don't you see that I am going through withdrawal? I need sordidness! I want to be told to put my arms up against the wall! Can't you see that if the institution turns out to be human, then *I* am the monster?

I Am Myself and My Prohibitions

– There, right in front of the Norm . . . a little farther back . . . farther . . . good! Stay there, and keep looking up. Good! Another. . . . It's printing, now almost done. . . . It looks like you've been practicing this pose your whole life.

This is what the press photographer says to the artist during the shoot for a spread that will accompany an interview. The genre that the two participate in is one of the most successful and significant recent genres: *the portrait of the artist with prohibition*. The photo can also be a video, as in Cristina Lucas's *Habla* (2008), whose initial image shows the Spanish artist, shot from behind, wearing a black dress, with her hair tied back in a ponytail. In her right hand, she carries a hammer, and she walks forward – toward a marble reproduction of Michelangelo's *Moses*, which, it turns out, is an image that is even more powerful than the act of iconoclasm that the artist carries out, blow by blow, perched on the statue. More recently, and more like a model, Annette Messager looks into the camera, confronting us. She is shown before a white wall with numerous signs forbidding various acts. The installation is called *Les Interdictions* (2014), and its upper part consists of fifteen faceless dolls, lifeless in rompers, who hang from the first row of signs, as if the proliferation of red bars – diagonal red bars – had robbed them of their breath, their lives. By contrast, the French artist is radiant, powerful against this backdrop, this landscape of nos. One might even mistake her for *La Liberté guidant le peuple*.

No singing. This other sign, textual rather than iconic, still hangs on the walls of certain traditional places. It is one of the favorite motifs of the genre: Pilar Albarracín uses it when she shows herself dressed up in the *faralaes* of her native Seville, tied up and gagged in a dive bar decorated with posters of matadors, all presided over by a bull's head. This kind of satire of a hypermasculine space that implicitly excludes femininity can also be found in the portraits of Grayson Perry, who extends his critique to the field of queer identities. A biological male who presents as a dreamy young girl in this context, he reclaims the right to sing, to belt out the melody of a song about his migration, his journey across genders and ages. It is significant that the physical expressions of the models are not emphasized in either of these cases; these expressions do not reproduce the dramatic symbolism of situations. Instead it is as if a sort of calm came over the model, produced by the contrast between the body and its textual and scenic surroundings. Moreover, one often sees the subject of this kind of portrait in a relaxed, comfortable state, like the smiling Alicia Framis, sitting Indian style in *The Room of Forbidden Books* (2004), one of her ephemeral, cubicle constructions. Here, on the shelves of a cushioned room, she has arranged a library made up of books that are or have been censored. The welcoming, secluded space lends the word *well-being* a new meaning, in a context in which permanent crisis seems to have banished well-being. Here it means: finding spiritual peace, surrounded by censorship.

Alice Framis, *The Room of Forbidden Books*, 2004
(© Blueproject Foundation).

In the history of artistic self-representation,
this model has a precedent in another form,
developed during the last century and repeated
so often that it became a sort of ID card for good
avant-garde artists: the self-portrait of the artist at
home with "primitive" objects hung on the wall
behind him. The tribal mask, the idol – such an
enigma – and other religious fixtures extracted
from the heart of darkness would serve to indicate decoratively a key feature of the painter's
character. The colonial, Africanist commitment
to seeking out ritual, magic, and the purity of
the unlettered in "precivilized" lands: all of this

lent the artist an aura of the taboo. In the absence of accurate information about the objects' provenance, function, and meaning, these archaic forms could all signify the same thing: the law of sacred and primordial terror. But these images belong to the past. In our decolonial times, artists no longer pose in this Eurocentric fashion in front of statues about which they know nothing. And at the height of fourth-wave feminism, the body that best represents this sort of confrontation with the forbidden is no longer masculine. This is what has given rise to another, more current dichotomy between Freedom and the No.

On the Norm Considered as One of the Applied Arts, or The Adventures of a Gastronaut and an Epicurean

During the course of his studies of classical Rome, Foucault noted with surprise that in every text he consulted there were far fewer references to intimate relations than to food.[14] If you look up, you too will see that – who would have guessed – we have been becoming ever more Roman in this sense. On the one hand, the globalized iconosphere has made pornography so accessible and omnipresent that it has lost its singularity and its scopic status, and with them its psychic impact and implications. Integrated into a visual system dedicated to producing documents, freed from large industries and intermediaries, porn has ceased to be a radiant exception in the audiovisual imaginary and has become a mere technique for the multimedia documentation of human coupling. Meanwhile, genitality has ceased to be a primordial element in the definition of identity. For a long time, *the truth at the beating heart of sex*, a political, characterological, and social truth, kept humanity very entertained. And indeed it still offers moments of psychosexual entertainment. Some, sure. But . . . we are in the twenty-first century, and, after all, it's only sex. It's not food.

Because it turns out that suddenly the desire for truth has migrated from the genitals to the palate. Chefs have ceased to be mere employees in kitchens; they have made the words *avant-garde* and *deconstruction* their own. At a moment when the field of aesthetics had already renounced these words, chefs were invited to the Venice Biennale, and they learned to say in interviews what painters had always said: "It's about awakening sensations." "I can't explain how I do it." "It's an instinctive process." Ferran Adrià was photographed for a magazine, surrounded by tiny colored boxes with spices and other ingredients, in a visual homage to Pollock's most famous portrait. Food photography is no longer a degraded form of photography; now photographs of food have begun to fill exhibition halls, even while every owner of a smartphone can take and share close-ups of the delicacies that have become the clearest indices of living your best life.

With the cultural turn in tourist industries, local food products have ceased to be displayed as curiosities or bits of local color and have instead become proper cultural experiences. The applied arts have realized their potential to be perceived and consumed as Arts. Residents were rediscovered, with their cuisine, their lives arranged in a pseudo-local scene, a *trompe-l'oeil* of local color in which cultural experience no longer takes the form of visits to worn-out monuments and venerable architectural sites. Graffiti artists are now the painterly guides to every town. After a phase of exhaustion, when it fell into disfavor, reduced by the rise of conceptualism to a matter of archaeology of or mere *passéism*, sculpture is reemerging thanks to new participatory projects: monoliths with LED screens, joyous video portraits showing the neighborhood residents, and giant books whose protagonists are not monarchs and soldiers, but rather you and me acting in our capacity as "spirits of the place." This is the real populism: sculptural demagogy.

And just as locals, answering open calls, have climbed onto pedestals and made their faces into busts, so the most exquisite foods have ceased to be the stuff of class privilege. Being an epicure, a lover of fine food and drink, is no longer exceptional; it has become one more personality trait for the present. Low class, *haute cuisine*. On *MasterChef Junior*, even a kid can be one. Newspaper travel supplements, with their extensive reviews of bistros and "exquisite little holes in the wall," have become the real Culture publications. Those that still bear the latter name only consider those productions of the spirit that, alas, cannot be eaten, but can be enjoyed of an evening, before or after a meal, and can aid digestion, like *digestifs*.

Pansexualism has been replaced by *pan negro*, brown bread sold for six euros a slice.

In fact, the only object of consumption that can come anywhere near food, though without being able to compete with it, is poetry. Food and poetry share a compositional principle and process: synesthesia. Fused and alternating sensations: combined flavors, bittersweetness, remote memories recaptured, awakened by an unexpected ingredient. A memory that is activated, in a kind of anamnesis, in and through the work of the Genius of New Cuisine, anointed by flour and salt: Professor Emeritus of Saffron, Patron Saint of Frying Pans. This, and not the accessibility of social networks, is the cause of the unforeseen popularity of lyric poetry, poetry defined, *al modo romano*, as a cult of sensitivity, as in the ancient festivals, when one would eat, drink, and recite Catullus, whose poems were meant to be read aloud, to complement the pleasures of the palate, as well as some other pleasures. But those were secondary.

Don't Fuck. Eat Well.

Being polymorphously perverse, desiring everyone and everything, and being capable of a varied and developed sexual response to any stimulus:

Western civilization has commended this understanding of sexual liberation, from Freudianism to
the philosophy of desire and through to the hypersexual commercial practices of advertising firms.
This ideal is within reach for almost everyone. . . .
But in an age of work addiction, the will alone is
not enough to attain it. It takes a peculiar character, a personality type known as *hypersexual*.
Although more and more people adopt hypersexual behaviors even without embodying this
personality type, living the dream of the poly-
morphous, hypersensual body turns out to be as
difficult in bed as it is easy at the table. Cuisines
local and fusion, West–Eastern Diwan. A roc-
coco breakfast with oysters, snails with oxtail, the
delicious hermaphroditism of the shrimp. This is
normative diversity, orchestrated polymorphous-
ness, epicurean excess. "What would it mean,"
Jane Ward asks, "to think about people's capacity
to cultivate their own sexual desires, in the same
way we might cultivate a taste for food?"[15] This is
the utopian question of the future.

Don't say *sexy*. Say *foodie*.

Let's admit it: we've stopped giving sex all
the credit. The truth is no longer found in it.
Because of the hypertrophy of the norm, the

proliferation of taxonomies that have multiplied, metastasized. Because the workings of the rule and transgression have reached a point of saturation. For the same reason that there are no longer world-famous painters and art has lost the appeal that it had until the late twentieth century. Because although only a few things go, the idea that anything goes is now widespread, and this mantra, which sounds liberating, has in fact made the spectator feel orphaned and disoriented in a limbo without prohibitions. As soon as the last academic norm lost its validity, the public rushed out of the museum, looking for another place in which to watch the pantomime that pits the censor against the liberator. They found it in the kitchen, where norms, although they are as strict as those in force in any other place, have not yet led to a universally accepted nomography, a hierarchical separation between the gourmet, the aficionado, and the layperson. Not yet. But in every high-end trough, in every satiated stomach, and in the heavenly palate that there is in every mouth, we find the key ingredients of a law and of a form.

Notes

Grey Alert, Blue Pill

1 Boris Vian, *Vercoquin et le plancton*, Madrid: Impedimenta, 2010, 105–7.
2 Gaby Bess, *Post pussy*, Almería: El Gaviero, 2015, 9.
3 Guy Baret, *Éloge de l'héterosexualité*, Paris: Les Belles Lettres, 1994, 27.
4 Alain Naze, *Manifeste contre la normalisation gay*, Paris: La Fabrique, 2017. See also Lee Edelman, *No Future*, Durham, NC: Duke University Press, 2004.
5 Bess, *Post pussy*, 68.

The Nomographic Imagination

1 Avram J. Holmes and Lauren M. Patrick. "The Myth of Optimality in Clinical Neuroscience," *Trends in Cognitive Sciences*, 22 (3), 2018: 241–57.

2 Carlos Castilla del Pino, *Teoría de los sentimientos*, Barcelona: Tusquets, 2008, 192–8.

3 Christine M. Korsgaard, *The Sources of Normativity*, Cambridge: Cambridge University Press, 1996, 7–49.

4 Howard Becker, *Outsiders: Studies in the Sociology of Deviance*, New York: The Free Press, 1963, 148.

5 Juan Luis Moraza, *Ornamento y Ley*, Murcia: CENDEAC, 2007, 48–50.

6 Kathy Acker, *Blood and Guts in High School*, New York: Grove Press, 1978, 134.

7 *Translator's Note*: Here Porta plays with the phrase "*a lo hecho, pecho*," which means, among other things, "what's done is done." The title of this section in the original is "*a lo hecho, derecho*."

8 Becker, *Outsiders*.

9 Jean Bergeret, *La personnalité normale et pathologique*, Barcelona: Gedisa, 1996, 45–8.

10 *Translator's Note*: Here the author writes the word for "affairs," or simply "things," as follows: "©Os@s."

11 Michel Foucault, *Abnormal: Lectures at the Collège de France, 1974–1975*, trans. Graham Burchell, ed. Valerio Marchetti and Antonella Salomoni, London: Verso, 2003, 50.

12 Georges Canguilhem, *On the Normal and the Pathological*, trans. Carolyn R. Fawcett, London; D. Reidel, 1978, 152. See also Pierre Macherey, "Subjectivité et normativité chez Canguilhem et Foucault," in *La philosophie au sens large*, 2016, *https:// philolarge.hypotheses.org/1750#more-1750*.

13 Jacques Derrida, *Before the Law: The Complete Text of Préjugés*, trans. Sandra van Reenen and Jacques de Ville, Minneapolis: University of Minnesota Press, 2018, 39.

14 Derrida, *Before the Law*, 19.

15 Laurent de Sutter, *Après la loi*, Paris: PUF, 2018, 33–4.

16 Lauren Berlant, "Starved," in Janet Halley and Andrew Parker (eds.), *After Sex? On Writing Since Queer Theory*, Durham, NC: Duke University Press, 2011, 82.

17 Brot Bord, "*Somewhere Over the Rainbow*: Mercantilización y asimilación de la disidencia sexual," in Miriam Solá and Elena Urko (eds.), *Transfeminismos*, Orkoien: Txalaparta, 2013, 153–64.

18 José Luis Pardo, "La invasión de los cuerpos vivientes," in *Estética de lo peor*, Madrid: Pasos perdidos/Baratraria, 2011, 108.

19 Canguilhem, *On the Normal and the Pathological*, 148.

20 Michel Foucault, "The Genealogy of the Modern Individual," in *Michel Foucault: Beyond Structuralism and Hermeneutics*, ed. Hubert L. Dreyfus and Paul Rabinow, Chicago: University of Chicago Press, 1983, 171–2.

21 Canguilhem, *On the Normal and the Pathological*, 149.

22 Jean Maisonneuve and Marilou Bruchon-Schweitzer, *Modèles du corps et psychologie esthétique*, Buenos Aires: Paidós, 1984, 201ff.

23 Berlant, "Starved," 82; emphasis added.

24 Georges Perec, *Thoughts of Sorts*, trans. David Bellos, London: Notting Hill Editions, 2011.

Why Do They Call It "Sex"
When They Mean "the Ethical Dimension of the
Doctrine of Relation"?

1 Eve Kosofsky Sedgwick, *Epistemology of the Closet*, Berkeley: University of California Press, 1990, 25.

2 Vicent Andrés Estellés, *Horacianes*, LXXX in *Obra completa*, Vol. V: *Cant temporal*, Valencia: Edicions Tres i Quatre, 1980.

3 Michel Foucault, *The Punitive Society: Lectures at the Collège de France, 1972–1973*, trans. Graham Burchell, ed. Bernard Harcourt, Basingstoke: Palgrave Macmillan, 2000, 115.

4 Gabriela Wiener, *Sexographies*, trans. Lucy Greaves and Jennifer Adcock, Brooklyn: Restless Books, 2008, 44.

5 Harold Jaffe, *Sex for the Millennium*, Normal, IL: Black Ice/FC2, 1999, 149.

No One's Style

1 Noël Coward, *Semi-Monde*, London: Bloomsbury, 2014, 18.

2 Noël Coward, *Private Lives*, New York: Samuel French, Inc., 1930, 14.

3 Max Grobe, "From 'Seinfeld' to Steve Jobs: What Was Normcore & What Is It Now?," *Highsnobiety*, April 25, 2019, *https://www.highsnobiety.com/p/what-is-normcore/*.

4 Georg Simmel, "Fashion," *American Journal of Sociology* 62 (6), 1957: 552, 549. The case of denim offers

one example of such conscious neglect, which can also be thought of as anti-fashion. See Jorge Lozano, "Simmel: La moda, el atracitvo formal del límite," in Georg Simmel, *Filosofía de la moda*, Madrid: Casimiro, 2014, 23.

5 Giuseppe Scaraffia, "Eccentricità," in *Dizionario del dandy*, Palermo: Sellerio, 2007.

6 K-Hole, *Youth Mode: A Report on Freedom*, k-hole.net, 2013, 28, *http://khole.net/issues/youth-mode/*.

Desigual, or Difference

1 Rafael Cansinos-Assens, *Ética y estética de los sexos*, Madrid: Júcar, 1973, 160.

2 Judith Butler, *Undoing Gender*, New York: Routledge, 2004, 41.

3 Judith Butler, *Gender Trouble: Feminism and the Subversion of Identity*, New York: Routledge, 1990, 134.

4 Council of Europe, *Convention on Preventing and Combating Violence Against Women and Domestic Violence*, 2011, Chapter III.1, 16.

5 Drieu Godefridi, *La loi du genre*, Paris: Les Belles Lettres, 2015, 13–16.

6 Canguilhem, *On the Normal and the Pathological*, 148.

7 Jonathan Ned Katz, *The Invention of Heterosexuality*, Chicago: University of Chicago Press, 2007, 52.

On the Norm Considered as One of the Fine Arts

1 Canguilhem, *On the Normal and the Pathological*, 147.

2 Sigmund Freud, "The Moses of Michelangelo," in *The Standard Edition of the Complete Psychological Works of Sigmund Freud*, Vol. XIII, *1913–1914: Totem and Taboo and Other Works*, ed. James Strachey et al., London: Hogarth Press, 1955, 233.

3 Judith Butler, *Bodies that Matter: On the Discursive Limits of "Sex,"* New York: Routledge, 1993, 122.

4 Juan Vicente Aliaga, *Orden fálico*, Madrid: Akal, 2010, 204.

5 Jacques Derrida, *Spurs: Nietzsche's Styles*, trans. Barbara Harlow, Lincoln: University of Nebraska Press, 1978, 101.

6 Jacques Derrida, "Force of Law: The 'Mystical Foundation of Authority,'" trans. Mary Quaintance, in Drucilla Cornell, Michael Rosenfeld, and David Gray Carlson (eds.), *Deconstruction and the Possibility of Justice*, New York: Routledge, 1992, 23.

7 See Gore Vidal's comments in the documentary *The Celluloid Closet* (1995), directed by Rob Epstein and Jeffrey Friedman.

8 Judith Butler, *The Psychic Life of Power: Theories in Subjection*, Stanford, CA: Stanford University Press, 1997, 87.

9 The modern model is Friedrich Dürrenmatt's *The Visit* (1956), whose influence extends to films like *The Distinguished Citizen* (2016), directed by Gastón Duprat and Mariano Cohn.

10 Jean Dubuffet, *Prospectus et tous écrits suivants*, Barcelona: Barral, 1975, 125.

11 Luis Camnitzer, "My Museums," in *On Art, Artists, Latin America, and Other Utopias*, ed. Rachel Weiss, Austin: University of Texas Press, 2009, 114.

12 Xavier Rubert de Ventós, *Teoria de la sensibilitat*, Barcelona: Edicions 62, 1968, 213.

13 Boris Groys, *Art Power*, Cambridge, MA: MIT Press, 2008, 3. On installation and legislation, see Groys, "Poetics of Installation," in *Going Public*, New York: Sternberg, 2010, 51–69.

14 Michel Foucault, "On the Genealogy of Ethics: An Overview of a Work in Progress," in *Michel Foucault: Beyond Structuralism and Hermeneutics*, 229.

15 Brandon Ambrosino, "The Invention of Heterosexuality," March 16, 2017, *https://www.bbc.com/future/article/20170315-the-invention-of-heterosexuality*.